CAMBRIDGE LIBRARY COLLECTION

Books of enduring scholarly value

Religion

For centuries, scripture and theology were the focus of prodigious amounts
of scholarship and publishing, dominated in the English-speaking world
by the work of Protestant Christians. Enlightenment philosophy and
science, anthropology, ethnology and the colonial experience all brought
new perspectives, lively debates and heated controversies to the study of
religion and its role in the world, many of which continue to this day. This
series explores the editing and interpretation of religious texts, the history of
religious ideas and institutions, and not least the encounter between religion
and science.

Natural Theology

Specialising in optics and the motion of fluids, physicist George Gabriel Stokes
(1819–1903) was Lucasian Professor of Mathematics at Cambridge for over
fifty years, President of the Royal Society, Master of Pembroke College and the
most prominent religious scientist of his age. First published in 1893, *Natural
Theology* contains the text of ten lectures he gave at Edinburgh. Stokes favoured
the design argument for the existence of a Christian god, arguing against
Darwinism. He believed the Bible to be true, though at times metaphorical. The
lectures move from substantive observations on cosmology, electricity, gravity,
ocular anatomy and evolution through to *non sequiturs* regarding providential
design, human exceptionalism, the supernatural, spiritual immortality, and
Christ's dual materiality and divinity. Fossilising a moment of impending shift
in the history of ideas, these lectures highlight an intellectual dissonance in the
Victorian scientific establishment.

T0381855

Cambridge University Press has long been a pioneer in the reissuing of out-of-print titles from its own backlist, producing digital reprints of books that are still sought after by scholars and students but could not be reprinted economically using traditional technology. The Cambridge Library Collection extends this activity to a wider range of books which are still of importance to researchers and professionals, either for the source material they contain, or as landmarks in the history of their academic discipline.

Drawing from the world-renowned collections in the Cambridge University Library and other partner libraries, and guided by the advice of experts in each subject area, Cambridge University Press is using state-of-the-art scanning machines in its own Printing House to capture the content of each book selected for inclusion. The files are processed to give a consistently clear, crisp image, and the books finished to the high quality standard for which the Press is recognised around the world. The latest print-on-demand technology ensures that the books will remain available indefinitely, and that orders for single or multiple copies can quickly be supplied.

The Cambridge Library Collection brings back to life books of enduring scholarly value (including out-of-copyright works originally issued by other publishers) across a wide range of disciplines in the humanities and social sciences and in science and technology.

Natural Theology

*The Gifford Lectures Delivered Before
the University of Edinburgh in 1893*

GEORGE GABRIEL STOKES

CAMBRIDGE
UNIVERSITY PRESS

CAMBRIDGE UNIVERSITY PRESS

Cambridge, New York, Melbourne, Madrid, Cape Town,
Singapore, São Paolo, Delhi, Mexico City

Published in the United States of America by Cambridge University Press, New York

www.cambridge.org
Information on this title: www.cambridge.org/9781108053761

© in this compilation Cambridge University Press 2013

This edition first published 1893
This digitally printed version 2013

ISBN 978-1-108-05376-1 Paperback

This book reproduces the text of the original edition. The content and language reflect
the beliefs, practices and terminology of their time, and have not been updated.

Cambridge University Press wishes to make clear that the book, unless originally published
by Cambridge, is not being republished by, in association or collaboration with, or
with the endorsement or approval of, the original publisher or its successors in title.

NATURAL THEOLOGY

By the same Author.

NATURAL THEOLOGY.

THE GIFFORD LECTURES, 1891.

CROWN 8vo. PRICE 3s 6d.

NATURAL THEOLOGY

The Gifford Lectures

DELIVERED BEFORE THE UNIVERSITY OF
EDINBURGH IN 1893

BY

PROF. SIR G. G. STOKES, BART.,

LONDON
ADAM AND CHARLES BLACK
1893

CONTENTS

LECTURE I

LECTURE II

LECTURE III

LECTURE IV

LECTURE V

LECTURE VI

LECTURE VII

LECTURE VIII

LECTURE IX

LECTURE X

GIFFORD LECTURES

LECTURE I

Freer introduction of scientific subjects and Christian doctrines— Illustrations of the immense distances of the heavenly bodies —Their visibility implies a connection of some kind—Corpuscular and undulatory theories of light — Triumph of the latter, and evidence of the existence of the luminiferous ether—Which, nevertheless, is not recognisable by our senses —Its connection with electricity—Possibly with gravitation —Unexpected constitution of ether indicated by the phenomena of polarisation—The history of the theory of light warns us against a summary rejection of what seems inexplicable by natural causes.

IN commencing my second course of Gifford Lectures, I feel that I ought, in the first instance, to make my apologies to the University for the delay which has occurred, as they ought properly to have been given in my second year of office. I have next to express my thanks to the Senatus of the University for having accepted a proposal I made when it was too late in the past academical year to lecture at a time suited to the wants of the University, that

1

I should be allowed to deliver them during the present year instead. I come before you therefore to-day, not as actual, but as *ex*-Gifford Lecturer. I find that the arrangements which the University authorities had made with my successor are of such a nature that I trust no serious inconvenience will arise from the change, and I do not think there is anything in it that can be distasteful to or uncourteous towards the present holder of the office.

At the conclusion of my former course of Gifford Lectures, I expressed the intention, in case it should fall to me to deliver another course, of dealing more freely with subjects to which I had myself paid more special attention,—I mean scientific subjects in so far as they might appear to aid us in the theme to which the attention of the Lecturer is directed by the will of the Founder.[1] I said also that I should allow myself greater liberty in referring to distinctively Christian doctrines, not with the purpose of entering on the subject of Christian evidences, which would be quite foreign to the foundation, still less of engaging in polemical theology, which is expressly prohibited, but of pointing out what it is that is really involved, and that as a rule runs throughout the belief of Christendom. And surely if

---

[1] An extract from Lord Gifford's Will, showing his object in founding the lectureships, and the qualifications and duties of the lecturers, is printed at the end of the volume.

Christianity does not destroy, but supplement and fulfil, those seekings after God, those endeavours to methodise the principles of right conduct, which may be made by the exercise of the powers with which man is endowed, it cannot be reasonable to exclude all reference to Christian teaching, nor can I imagine that Lord Gifford intended that it should be thus excluded.

I have reason to think that the expression of an intention to bring before you rather matters that had occupied my attention than those which were new to me, and which I could only offer you at second hand, was received with favour; and in part fulfilment of my expressed intention I propose to-day to direct your attention to some questions connected with our present scientific knowledge.

It would not, however, be lawful for me, as Gifford Lecturer, to deliver to you a scientific lecture merely as such, and on account of the scientific interest of the subject that may be treated. But if we look on the framing of the material universe, the replenishing of the earth with living things, the formation of man with all his intellectual powers, his endowment with the sense of right and wrong, and generally with moral faculties—if, I say, we look on these as the work of a supreme Author of nature, then we may expect to find some general rules, or at least some analogies, running through even dissimilar portions of His work. It is conceivable that, even in the study of inanimate nature, we may get hints as to God's moral government of His rational creatures. But to perceive such hints it is not necessary to go through the various branches of Natural Science. Nothing more than hints of the most general kind as regards moral science need be expected from a subject so different as natural science; and such, if they are attainable, we might expect to find rather in what is common to different branches of natural science than in what is distinctive of some one branch.

By way of introduction to the subject which I propose to bring before you to-day, I wish to say a few words to help to give some idea which we can actually realise of the distances of the heavenly bodies. Statements regarding these distances are indeed to be found in every elementary text-book dealing with such subjects; but it is one thing to accept such statements as true, on the authority of those whom we believe to be competent to make such statements on grounds which we cannot in the least comprehend, and another to be able to form some idea of the sort of evidence on which the statements depend.

Now it requires no stretch of imagination to conceive that we should be able to make out the general form and the dimensions of the earth on

which we live. We travel long distances along it;
we can sail round it. To describe the refined
methods by which its dimensions are most accurately
ascertained, would lead me altogether too far from
my subject. Suffice it to say, that it is thoroughly
well proved to be very nearly spherical, with a
radius of about 4000 miles.

The heavenly bodies are not, however, accessible
to us. How then can we imagine their distances
from us to be measured? To form a conception of
this, suppose that we wished to ascertain the distance
of some inaccessible object on the earth's surface,
such as a rock a long way out at sea, we ourselves
being confined to a small island. Let us take two
stations on the island, some way apart, and so
chosen that they are visible from each other, and the
rock visible from both, and also that the distance
between them can be measured, suppose by a chain.
At each station we can observe the angle between
the directions of the other station and of the rock,
and thus in the triangle formed by the three objects,
as we have measured the base and the angles at the
base, we can calculate the sides, which are the
distances of the rock from the two stations.

If our supposed island were of very small dimensions, and the rock a very long way off, our triangle
would be so slender that, unless the two observed
angles were measured with very great precision, our

result could claim no great accuracy, though even in that case we *should* be able to affirm that the distance of the rock was *at least* as great as so and so.

Now we may endeavour by a somewhat similar operation to determine the distance of the heavenly bodies. In this case the earth on which we live takes the place of our small island, and by choosing two stations widely separated on the earth's surface we may procure a base of some thousands of miles. It is true that in this case the stations are not visible from each other; but as they are on known points on the terrestrial globe, the dimensions of which we know, it can be imagined that by suitable calculations, combined with observations of the heavenly body, which takes the place of the rock out at sea in our illustration, it might be possible to arrive at a definite result as to the distance of the body in question.

By methods of which the preceding illustration may serve to give a general idea, the distance has been ascertained of our nearest neighbour, the moon, which proves to be about a quarter of a million of miles. Already we have arrived at a distance which we hardly realise without reference to something with which we are more familiar to aid our conceptions. We are familiar with railway trains, and it may help us to reflect that it would take an express

train, travelling without stopping night or day, eight
months or so, to get over the distance from the earth
to the moon.

If we attempt to ascertain the distance of the
sun by the direct application of similar methods, we
find it to be so great as to prevent us from obtaining
trustworthy measurements of it. But by indirect
methods, still depending on the dimensions of the
earth for a base line, it has been ascertained that the
distance of the sun is about 92,000,000 miles—about
400 times the distance of the moon.

The distances of the stars are so enormous, that no
methods founded on the direct employment of the
distance between two points on the earth's surface as
a base line would lead to any positive result. But
in the course of a year the earth revolves round the
sun in an orbit which is nearly circular, with a
radius of 92,000,000 miles. It is conceivable that
though we failed to observe any appreciable displacement in the direction of a star according as it was
viewed from one side or the other of the earth on
which we live, yet if we were to observe it from two
points separated by such an enormous distance as
the diameter of the earth's orbit, some appreciable
change in the star's direction might be perceptible,
which might enable us to ascertain its distance from
the sun, the centre of our system. In point of fact,
such changes of direction have been ascertained to

exist in the case of some of the stars, but so excessively minute that, even in the case of α Centauri,
which so far as we know at present is our nearest
neighbour among the fixed stars, the concluded
distance of the star is so great that if the earth's
orbit round the sun could be seen from the star, it
would not appear as large as a threepenny piece seen
at the distance of a mile. And we have every
reason to believe that there are multitudes of stars
vastly more distant than that.

In spite of these almost inconceivably great
distances, the fact that we do see the stars shows
that there must be a connection of some kind
between us and them. It does not at once show that
light is of the nature of a messenger conveying to
us information respecting the star; for the word
"messenger" carries with it the idea of something
travelling; and it is conceivable that the influence of
the stars on us, which results in our seeing them,
might have nothing to do with progress from place
to place, but might be instantaneous. Nevertheless,
long before the distance of any of the stars had been
even approximately measured, two perfectly independent astronomical phenomena had revealed to us
the finiteness of the velocity of light, and had
enabled us to determine it. I allude, of course, to
an observed inequality, as it is called, or periodic
variation, in the observed times of occurrence of the

eclipses of Jupiter's satellites, and to a remarkable apparent annual displacement of the stars called aberration. These two phenomena fall so completely into their places, and the values of the velocity of light determined in two such utterly different ways agree so well together, that no doubt can remain that the professed explanation which refers them to the finite velocity of light is indeed the true explanation. And within the last half-century the velocity of light, notwithstanding its enormous magnitude, has been actually determined experimentally in terms of measured distances in the neighbourhood of the station of observation, or even in the room in which the experiment was made, and a value obtained for the velocity which closely agrees with those given by the two celestial phenomena. In these ways we now know that the velocity of light is a little over 186,000 miles per second. Vast as this rate is, corresponding to the passage over a distance exceeding seven times the circumference of the earth in one second, it yet would take about three and a half years for light to travel from α Centauri to us ; and this reference to the velocity of light aids us in conceiving the enormous distance of even the nearest of the stars.

Now there are two, and as far as I can see, only two, possible ways in which we can conceive of the transmission of such a message: either we must

have something darted forth with this enormous
velocity from the body from which the light comes,
or a certain change of condition must be propagated
in a medium already existing, if not in infinite space,
at least as far as the remotest visible star. These
two radically different conceptions lie at the base of
the two rival theories of light which, for a long time,
divided the allegiance of men of science—namely,
the corpuscular theory, or theory of emission, and
the theory of undulation. The former, supported as
it was by the great name of Newton, was for a long
time that most in vogue. But subsequent researches
have brought to light such an overwhelming amount
of evidence in favour of the theory of undulations,
that there cannot be a moment's hesitation which
alternative we must adopt as to the nature of light;
and at the present day the statement that light
consists in undulations may be regarded as one of
the certainly ascertained results of scientific inquiry.

The undulatory theory demands of necessity the
existence of some sort of *medium*, as it is called,
extending at least to the remotest star, and existing
likewise within such bodies as glass, water, etc. It
would take me much too far from my subject to
enter into the arguments, on the strength of which
we conclude that this medium (to which the name
of *luminiferous ether* has been given) exists within
ponderable bodies, as well as in free space.

And yet this hypothetical medium, the ether, is a thing of which our senses give us no direct cognisance. We cannot feel it, or smell it, or weigh it, and yet we have overwhelming evidence that it exists. And one most important object which it fulfils is that of informing us of objects at a distance through the sense of sight. But its functions do not cease here. There is the strongest reason for believing that heat in the radiant form—heat as furnished to us in the rays of the sun—is identical in its physical nature with light, not differing from what we call light, otherwise than as light of one colour differs from light of another. Just consider for a moment in what condition our earth would be if it received no heat from the sun. The earth all over would be in a worse condition for warmth than is the highest latitude that Arctic explorers have reached, even in the depth of the northern winter. No vegetation could go on, nor could we avail ourselves of coal fires, for coal is the remains of vegetation in remote geological ages. And even if we had coal fires, the warmth which we at present experience in standing before them would be unknown, for that heat is conveyed to us by radiation from the fire.

Though the conveyance of light and of heat in the radiant form constitute those offices of the luminiferous ether on which we can most definitely lay, as it were, our finger, we can hardly suppose that it has

not other functions to fulfil. One of the most striking discoveries of modern times we owe to your
countryman, the late Professor Clerk Maxwell.
Among the agents around us which we render sub-
servient to our wants, one of the most mysterious
is electricity. We employ it in electroplating, in
lighting our streets and apartments, in sending messages, we may say instantaneously, to distant parts
of the earth; we employ it as a motor power, in
many cases specially convenient, at least for small
machines, though its applicability is not limited to
small machines, but it is in some cases used in
propelling carriages on railways. And yet, for all
this, we are unable to give a definite answer to the
question, What is electricity ? What is the precise
meaning of an electric current, or of a charge of
statical electricity ? But though we are ignorant of
the nature of electricity, though we are unable to
affirm as much of it as we do of light, when we say
light consists in undulations, yet we are able to
investigate the laws of electricity, and subject the
phenomena which it presents to us to refined mathematical analysis, and to compare with great accuracy
the conclusions of theory with observation. Now
Maxwell showed that two fundamental constants
relating to electricity, the ratio of which, from the
nature of the case, represents some velocity, and
which are capable of numerical determination by

laboratory experiments, were so related that the velocity in question was, within the limits of errors of observation, equal to the velocity of propagation of light.
This formed the starting-point of his electromagnetic
theory of light, according to which light consists in
the propagation of an electromagnetic disturbance.
This theory has quite recently received a remarkable confirmation through the investigations of
Professor Hertz, who has succeeded in showing, by
purely electrical means, that an electromagnetic
disturbance, such as was previously known through
Faraday's discovery of electromagnetic induction,
was capable of reflection and interference just like
light. As with light, so here the phenomena of
interference furnish data for determining the length
of a wave. The values so determined come out,
indeed, of altogether a different order of magnitude
from what we had been used to in the study of
light. Instead of wave-lengths ranging about the
50,000th part of an inch, we have such as are to be
measured by yards, or feet, or inches at the very
least. But such a difference in the scale of magnitude, great though it be, is no proof of a diversity
of physical nature; and though the light of lowest
refrangibility that affects our eyes has still a wave-
length of say the $\frac{1}{35000}$ of an inch, we know that
there are radiations extending downwards much below
the extreme red, and capable of detection by their

heating or their photographic effects; and to these rays belong wave-lengths considerably larger than any that affect the eye, though still, it is true, comparable in magnitude with the waves of light rather than with the electromagnetic waves with which Hertz worked. But though this extension of wave-length indicated by phenomena, which had long been identified in their physical nature with light, leaves us still far from reaching those attained by purely electromagnetic means, still, as I said, the mere difference of magnitude is no valid argument against an identity of nature—an identity so strongly supported by the community of laws in the two phenomena. On the whole, there appears to be little doubt that the luminiferous ether is in some way intimately concerned in the phenomena of electricity, though the nature of electricity itself, and of its various manifestations, is a matter still veiled in mystery. And as electricity, in some of its aspects, is closely connected with chemical action, we are led to speculate on some connection which we do not understand between the luminiferous ether and chemical affinity, and with the all-important results which depend upon it.

There is yet another direction towards which our thoughts are turned in speculating on the various offices which the luminiferous ether may fulfil. Newton's great discovery of universal gravitation

has reduced to law, and enabled us to predict by
mathematical calculation, the complicated movements
of the bodies of the solar system. But what is gravitation in itself? How is it that two bodies at a distance, suppose the moon and the earth, are drawn
towards one another; or, to come nearer home, why
is it that an apple, detached from the bough on which
it hung, falls to the earth? This is a question which
we are not able to answer; but as to what gravitation is not, Newton himself has used very strong
language. In the course of a letter to Bentley, he
says: "That gravity should be innate, inherent, and
essential to matter, so that one body may act upon
another at a distance through a *vacuum*, without the
mediation of anything else, by and through which
their action and force may be conveyed from one to
another, is to me so great an absurdity, that I believe
no man who has, in philosophical matters, a competent faculty of thinking, can ever fall into it.
Gravity must be caused by an agent acting constantly according to certain laws; but whether this
agent be material or immaterial, I have left to the
consideration of my readers." I suppose the alternative which Newton had in his mind, and left to the
consideration of his readers, was a theory somewhat
analogous to the corpuscular theory of light (such,
for example, as Le Sage's theory of ultramundane
corpuscles), or some theory in so far analogous to

the undulatory theory of light, as that the effect is referred to something already existing in the space which separates the attracting bodies. The over-whelming evidence which, at the present time, exists in favour of the undulatory theory of light, proves that there *is* something intervening in the space which separates attracting bodies, and the tendency, I think, is to lead us to suppose that the luminiferous ether is in some way, which we do not understand, the link of connection, whereby bodies at a distance are enabled to attract one another with the attraction of gravitation.

As this ether is not directly recognisable by us by means of our senses in the manner of ponderable matter, it will readily be understood that its properties may, in great measure, remain unknown to us, or be only in part arrived at by induction from observed phenomena. When the idea was seriously entertained of explaining the properties of light by the supposition that light consisted in the undulations of a subtle medium, men's thoughts naturally turned to the analogy of sound. Sound, which we know to consist in an undulatory motion propagated through the air, exhibits many phenomena, such, for example, as reflection, refraction, interference, analogous to the corresponding phenomena in light; and the luminiferous ether would naturally have been regarded as a fluid, elastic in the same sense as air, but vastly more subtle. The undulations which constitute light would naturally be supposed to arise from condensations and rarefactions, just as in the case of air. At a distance from the body which is the source of sound, we know that the vibrations of the air are to and fro in the direction in which the sound is propagated, and such would naturally be supposed to be the case with light. But though, as I have said, light and sound exhibit many features in common, there are some phenomena in light which have absolutely no counterpart in sound; I allude more especially to double refraction and polarisation. Hygens, to whom we owe the discovery of the laws of double refraction as exhibited in Iceland spar, had nearly finished his treatise on the subject when he discovered the phenomenon of polarisation, closely bound up though it be with that of double refraction. What the appropriate idea of polarised light could be remained a mystery, and the phenomena which Hygens observed in connection with polarisation fitted ill with the notions which he had been led to entertain respecting the cause of double refraction. For considerably more than a century after Hygens' discovery of polarisation, that modification of light was unknown, save as a result of, or at least in direct connection with, double refraction. But early in the present century Malus made the important discovery that the very same modification of light,

2

designated by the term polarisation, could be conferred on it simply by reflection at a proper angle
from glass and various other substances; in fact,
transparent substances generally, though not (except
it be partially and very imperfectly) by metals.
Hence polarisation must be some modification of
light which exists quite independently of double
refraction, though, as the connection of the two
phenomena shows, the cause of double refraction
must have an intimate relation to polarisation, whatever that may be. But it was not for many years
after this discovery that the appropriate idea was
suggested of what it was that constituted polarisation. Dr. Young seems to have been the first to
suggest it; though shortly afterwards Fresnel, who
had been engaged along with Arago in an experimental investigation of the laws of interference of
polarised light, placed the theory of polarisation (by
which I mean the theory of what it is that constitutes
polarisation, not a theory of the manner in which
that modification of light is brought about) on, we
may say, an irrefragable basis. It was shown that
in polarised light the vibrations, instead of being to
and fro in the direction of propagation, must be
transverse to that direction; and, as a consequence,
that in ordinary light they must take place in the
planes of the waves. This demanded a complete
revolution in the character of the elasticity which we

must attribute to the ether. It must consist in an elastic resistance to the gliding on of one layer over another, a sort of elasticity unknown in liquids or gases, though it occurs in elastic solids. How the ether can at the same time behave like an elastic solid in resisting the gliding of one portion over another, and yet like a fluid in letting bodies freely pass through it, is a mystery which we do not understand. Nevertheless, we are obliged to suppose that so it is. This shows how little right we have to presume upon our knowledge when we come to deal with a medium like the ether, of which our senses give us no direct cognisance.

In bringing before you the subject of the luminiferous ether, and the slow progress which man has made in getting some knowledge of its existence and properties, it may naturally have occurred to you to ask, What can all this have to do with the proper subject of the Gifford Lectures? I said, however, in my former Lectures, that if we regard the course of nature, inanimate, living, intellectual, moral, as all alike the work of the supreme Author of nature, we might expect to find, at least to some extent, a similarity of plan between one portion of His works and another; at least to the extent that we might obtain hints bearing on one branch of the subject, from the consideration of another apparently utterly

dissimilar. Let us see now whether lessons, bearing
even on a subject so apparently remote as natural
theology, may not be deduced from our study of the
phenomena which led up to our acceptance of the
existence of an ether endowed with properties which
we only very imperfectly understand, but which, as
far as we do understand them, are such as we should
never have dreamt of attributing to it *à priori.*

There is a strong tendency at the present day to
assume that all the phenomena which fall under our
notice are to be explained by the interaction of
forces such as those which we can examine or make
experiments with. Of course nobody can pretend
that we can actually so explain them; the tacit
assumption I refer to is that they are of a nature to
be so explained, so that any asserted fact respecting
which there does not appear to be the slightest probability that we could explain it by any means of
investigation open to us must therefore be rejected
as incredible.

Now the history of the progress of physical optics
affords a warning to us how fallacious such an assumption may be. The assumption to start with
that all space, or all at least of which we have any
cognisance, must be imagined to be completely filled
with a supposed medium of which our senses give us
no information, already makes, we might reasonably
say, a severe demand upon our credulity; and indeed

there are, or at least have been, minds to which the
demand appeared to be so great as to cause the
rejection of that theory of light. And when we
provisionally assume the existence of an ether, and
use it as a working hypothesis in our further investigations, we find ourselves obliged to admit properties
of this supposed ether so utterly different from what
we should have imagined beforehand, through our
previous experience, that we are half staggered, and
demand the fullest evidence before we can accept the
conclusions. Of course it is quite right that we
should demand full evidence. But it is a different
thing altogether to reject the theory which is asserted
to explain so much, merely because it runs counter
to much that we should confidently have anticipated
from our previous experience. Such a proceeding
may well be prejudicial to the progress of even
physical science. A slashing article in an old number
of the *Edinburgh Review*, ridiculing the supposed
vagaries of an undulationist, had probably the effect
of diminishing the share which our own country took
in the great revival of physical optics in the present
century.

In the case of the luminiferous ether, the evidence
by which we are ultimately led to believe in its
existence, and its possession of properties so different
from what we should have imagined beforehand, is
of course of a similar nature to that which meets us

in the study of other branches of physical science, where we have to do with bodies the existence of which is directly made known to us by the exercise of our senses. To this extent I grant the illustration is inadequate to represent precisely what it is intended to elucidate. Nevertheless, it does, I think, show how we may miss the truth if we set out with a determination to refuse a hearing to what professes to be truth, merely because we cannot imagine it to be established by evidence at all of the nature of that on the strength of which the results of the study of physical science are believed in, and because we have determined to attend to no other.

It will probably be perceived that the question to which my remarks are leading up is this—Are we justified in rejecting what is asserted as claiming belief on the ground of evidence in part at least professedly supernatural merely on the ground that it is supernatural? It is not my purpose to discuss, and indeed I am forbidden to lean upon, evidence of a supernatural nature. But it fairly belongs to the province of reason to investigate the question whether we are or are not justified in rejecting the supernatural merely as such.

But in order to avoid confusion, before attempting to answer this question we must ask another—What is meant by supernatural? Of course in one sense it may be claimed that nothing is supernatural. If

we include in nature all that is, then, of course, there
can be nothing supernatural. It is obvious that it
cannot be in this sense that the word is used. But
there is an ordinary course of nature with which we
are familiar: the sun rises and sets, the seasons
alternate, summer and winter, the matter around us
possesses such and such properties, which we investigate, and of whose action we determine the laws,
plants vegetate in a generally similar manner one
year to another   All this is according to the ordinary
course of nature, and we do not therefore speak of
it as supernatural. Again, changes are incessantly
effected which would never have been brought about
by the mere action of the natural forces about us,
but which depend upon the will of man, who chooses
to bring about such and such results, and sets to work
accordingly. But these too belong to the ordinary
familiar course of nature, and we do not speak of
them as supernatural.

But suppose it is asserted that something utterly
unlike the ordinary course of nature has occurred, so
unlike that we cannot imagine it to have taken place
through the action of the forces which we see around
us, or to have been the work of man, are we therefore
justified in rejecting the statement as absurd and
incredible? That depends upon whether we are
authorised in affirming that our minds and our
senses, taken together, are competent to undertake

the investigation of anything that may exist in nature. I say designedly " to undertake the investigation of," not " to investigate," for the expression " to investigate " might be supposed to mean, to make at least some little step towards the explanation ; whereas, what I mean, is to regard the subject as lying within our competence to attack with some chance of success. Now, if even in a purely physical science, like that of light, an obstinately conservative adherence to the conclusions supposed to be derived from our previous experience, and refusal to look beyond, would have caused us to miss the discovery of the splendid theory which now guides us so unerringly through a labyrinth of observed facts, it may well be that a proud assertion of our competence to enter on the investigation of all subjects by our own unaided powers will shut us out from the apprehension of truths of a different kind, which yet may be to us of the utmost importance.

The unreasonableness of any such *à priori* rejection of all that transcends the ordinary course of nature, such as we observe it, will be the more apparent on a little further consideration. The examination of what we see in nature, as I insisted on in my Lectures two years ago, presents us with problems as to origin which there does not seem to be the slightest chance of our being able to solve merely by reference to such natural causes as those that we are acquainted with. Take, for example, the problem of the origin of life ;

or again, take evolution itself, viewed in connection
with the physical evidence that the order of things
which we see about us, regarded in a wide sense, as
stretching over ages, is one not of periodicity but of
progress, negativing the idea that it can have existed
from a past eternity. We require some cause above
the ordinary laws of nature. Furthermore, the examination of nature presents us with overwhelming
evidence of design, but design is unintelligible without
a designing mind. But once we admit the existence
of an intelligent Author of nature, it would be absurd
to deny to Him the powers of free will, of origination,
which man himself possesses, and it would be in the
highest degree presumptuous to suppose that He is
limited by those natural laws under which alone man
can work. Hence it follows that we have no right
to reject as incredible everything that transcends the
order of nature as we observe it or could observe it.
But, of course, while we are not justified in proudly
rejecting the supernatural merely as such, we are not
to suppose that mere credulity is a virtue. We have
a right to demand that reasonable evidence shall be
afforded us of what we are called on to accept, even
though it lie outside the ordinary course of nature;
what we have not a right to do is to demand that that
evidence shall be of a particular kind, analogous to
the evidence by means of which we make progress in
the study of natural science.

Nor is it only in warning us against the summary rejection of what claims to be supernatural, that we may learn a lesson from the history of the theory of the luminiferous ether. It may be that our thoughts lead us to the conception of some agency at work, of which our senses give us no direct cognisance, and which is not open to our experimental investigation. We are not, therefore, authorised in summarily rejecting the supposition of its existence. In a future Lecture I shall have some speculations of this character to bring before you—speculations belonging to a sort of border-land between the natural and the supernatural. I do not profess that they are more than speculations, or claim for a moment that you should accept them ; all I can venture to ask is that you will kindly give me a hearing.

LECTURE II

Conception suggested by the properties of the ether of instantaneous
transmission of intelligence—Division of physical sciences into
distinct branches—Fundamental character of the laws of motion
—Yet to these must be superadded gravitation—And to these
again magnetism, etc.—Similarly the physical laws do not
suffice, but when we come to living things, fresh laws must be
superadded—Superficial character of certain resemblances in
inorganic nature to phenomena of life—Materialism and directionism—Reflex action and volition—Theological tendencies
of adoption or rejection of materialism.

I HAVE already brought before you the subject of the
luminiferous ether in one of its aspects—namely,
that of its mysterious nature, our senses giving us no
direct cognisance of its existence, while yet we have
the highest evidence in the present state of our
scientific knowledge that such a thing does really
exist. I would now refer to one of its properties, or
at least what we have very strong reason for believing to be one of its properties, and follow out some
trains of thought that thence arise.

The existence of the luminiferous ether was first
assumed on account of the prospect which it seemed
to hold out of explaining the existence and properties
of light. What an overwhelming amount of evidence

is available at the present day in favour of its existence, those only who have made a special study of
the subject are fully in a condition to judge.   In the
earlier progress of the science of physical optics, our
knowledge of the analogous phenomena of sound was
of immense assistance.   It is not, however, as a
vehicle for the propagation of light that I propose to
speak of the ether to-day, but rather in relation to
properties which we may suppose it to possess which
have not been brought out in observation, but which
are more closely analogous, if they exist, to the
properties of the air in relation to sound, than are
those of the ether in relation to light.   And it falls
in with my plan that I should, in the first instance,
direct your attention to sound rather than to light.

Sound, as we know, under ordinary circumstances
consists in a vibratory movement of the air, propagated from point to point by means of the elasticity
of the air, elasticity meaning the force whereby the
air resists change of volume; exercising a greater
pressure than in its undisturbed state when it is
compressed, and a smaller pressure when it is rarefied.   It travels in air of average temperature at the
rate of about 1100 feet per second.   It thus affords
us speedy information of things going on at a moderate,
or even some considerable distance from us.   The
distance at which a sound is audible naturally depends
on its intensity—on the amount, that is, of the

disturbance involved in it. A cannon shot may be heard to the distance of some miles. The most remarkable instance of the audibility of sound to great distances occurred in the case of the great eruption of Krakatoa in 1883. The sound of the explosion was heard even in Australia, where it was imagined that a naval engagement must have been going on at sea, and even as far off as Ceylon. When such long distances are concerned, the propagation is by no means what we should regard as sensibly instantaneous. Thus for sound to travel 750 miles would take about an hour.

When we are dealing with such violent disturbances, the actual excursions of the particles and the accompanying changes of pressure are not excessively small. Thus, in the Krakatoa explosion, a disturbance in the atmosphere of the same nature as that to which sound is due, but not audible, as being of too long a period, was traced in the records of self-recording barometers all over the world; and it even appears that this disturbance travelled round the earth to the antipodes of Krakatoa, where the disturbances coming in from all directions crossed, and actually went more than once round the earth again. But volcanic eruptions or the explosions of powder mills are comparatively rare; what I wish to direct your attention to, is the almost inconceivable minuteness of the disturbance of the air in the case

of sounds which, nevertheless, are easily audible.
Take an ordinary tuning-fork and strike it. The
sound given out is very feeble. But press the end of
the handle down on a table, and a clear, far louder
note is given out. Why is this? The reason is that,
in the first case, when the tuning-fork is immersed
in air, not in contact with any solid substance except
the soft flesh of the thumb and forefinger, between
which the handle is held, the prongs make indeed
very sensible excursions to and fro, as may be perceived by their slightly misty outline, the actual
vibrations being too rapid for the eye to follow; and,
of course, as either prong moves, it pushes the air out
of its way, or draws it in from behind by tending to
create a vacuum which is filled in from the adjacent
air. But in consequence of the small diameter in
any direction of a section of either prong, the air
which is pushed from the front can easily get round
to the rear, returning again in the second half of the
complete vibration, so that by far the greater part of
the motion of the air consists in a local reciprocating
motion from front to rear, taking place just as it
would in an incompressible fluid, and not being
accompanied by condensation and rarefaction, so that
hardly any sonorous vibration is produced. But
when the end of the handle is pressed against a table,
or better still, a sounding-board, the excessively
minute vibrations of the tip of the handle are com-

municated to the sounding-board; and as this presents
a broad, flat face to the air, this elastic fluid is unable
to escape to the rear, gets alternately condensed and
rarefied, and so sonorous vibrations are produced.
But the amount of excursion of the air cannot exceed
the excursion of the sounding-board, which is merely
microscopic in amount; and at some distance from
the tuning-fork the excursion of the air is still
further reduced, by the divergence of the disturbance,
and yet the sound is very well heard. We see in
this way how almost inconceivably minute may be
the actual amount of disturbance which yet is
competent to produce a very sensible sound.

Let us turn now from sound to light. The comparatively sluggish velocity of propagation of 1100
feet per second is exchanged for the enormous
velocity of upwards of 186,000 miles per second.
But this is not all. A study of the phenomena
of light led in time to the discovery that the
vibrations which constitute light could not be, as
we know is the case with sound, to and fro in
the direction in which the sound is propagated,
but must be transverse to the direction of propagation. This requires in the medium in which
the vibrations are propagated the existence of a
sort of elasticity whereby the medium resists dis-
tortion of figure, of a kind which does not involve
alteration of volume. It has been shown that an

elastic medium which is constituted alike in all directions possesses simultaneously two sorts of elasticity—one that whereby it opposes resistance to a change of volume, like air and other gases, the other the kind just mentioned; and that to these two kinds of elasticity correspond respectively two kinds of disturbance—one similar to that of air when propagating sound, the other that which has just been mentioned in relation to light. It has been shown further that in a medium possessing both kinds of elasticity—and such apparently must be the ether if indeed it acts mechanically—the velocity of propagation of the to-and-fro vibrations must be considerably, and may be enormously, greater than that of the transverse kind, which latter it is that constitute light. It has further been shown by Green, by a combination of dynamical conclusions with what we know of light, that in the case of the ether the normal vibrations, those analogous to the vibrations of the air in the case of sound, must be propagated incomparably more swiftly than the transversal vibrations which constitute light; with a velocity accordingly which, if finite at all, must at least be incomparably greater than one of 186,000 miles per second. These normal vibrations, if they exist, may conceivably afford a means of communication to enormous distances, at a rate which may be deemed instantaneous.

It appears then that the study of purely physical science leads us to the contemplation of the possibility of the communication of intelligence from one part of the universe to another, with a velocity so great that we are unable to assign any limit to it, while the means of communication are such as to involve only disturbances of inconceivable minuteness in an existing medium. Possibly this thought may help a little the minds of some by aiding them to conceive of an intelligent Will as pervading the whole universe. But in saying this, I wish to emphasise the expression I made use of just now— "leads us to the contemplation of"; for I should be sorry that any one should suppose that I was making the slightest attempt to give a physical explanation of a purely theological proposition.

The physical sciences are divided into distinct branches, some of which, partly perhaps in consequence of their being most obvious and longest known, we are disposed to regard as the more fundamental. Foremost among these may be placed the laws of motion, even though we cannot altogether say that a perfectly distinct idea of mass and its measurement was known from ancient times. I do not suppose that any clear conception of mass as distinguished from weight was attained to before the time of Newton. The fact, that in the observation

of the motion of matter, as we have it on the surface of
the earth on which we live, mass is so mixed up with
weight, tended somewhat to obscure the independent
conception of mass. Newton was the first to prove
that weight at a given place on earth was strictly
proportional to mass, which he did by experiments
on pendulums, which it would lead me much too far
from my subject to enter into. As I have already
remarked in my former course, we may easily, with
our present knowledge, place ourselves in conceivable circumstances in which we might have grown
up with a familiar idea of mass, and of the laws of
motion, and known nothing whatsoever of gravitation
We have only to imagine that we were born and
brought up on an excessively minute planet, so
small that its attraction of gravitation for the things
on its surface, our own bodies inclusive, would be
quite insensible. Supposing a rational and philo-
sophically-minded race of minute beings to have
lived on such a planet, they might have easily made
out the laws of motion, and have constructed an
elaborate system of dynamics, without knowing
anything whatsoever of the existence of weight or
gravitation. This mysterious property of gravitation, the effects of which, in the actual condition
of our lives, meet us at every turn, is accordingly
something which we must regard as superadded to
the mechanical properties of matter. It is true that

many have speculated on possible explanations of gravitation, which would reduce it to what I have called the mechanical properties of matter, but no one as yet has arrived at any satisfactory theory.

But even if we include gravitation in the mechanical properties of matter, that will by no means suffice for the explanation of the physical phenomena which are presented to us in our examination of inorganic nature. Take the properties of the lodestone, or of a steel bar which has been rubbed with it. We have here manifestations of attraction and repulsion, of setting in a particular direction in the case of a body free to turn without sensible friction about a vertical axis, which we can by no means refer to the mechanical properties of matter, even when we include gravitation among them. We are obliged to admit the existence of a wonderful something outside these properties, which we call magnetism. We cannot, of course, say that magnetism is incapable of explanation on purely mechanical principles, but assuredly we are not at all authorised to say that it is capable.

Again, take the phenomena presented by a rubbed piece of sealing-wax. Here, again, we have manifestations of attraction and repulsion wholly different from what are exhibited by magnets, and apparently having no connection with them. They are, I need not say, shown on a far larger scale in the frictional electrifying machine, and not merely phenomena of attraction and repulsion, but various others, such as the production of brilliant sparks, a shock to the system, and so forth.

Again, take the very common phenomenon of the burning of a candle. We have here a production of light and heat not referable, so far as we know, to the mechanical properties of matter, or to magnetism, or to electricity. We are introduced to what we are obliged to refer to something different, which we call chemical affinity. Of course it does not always show itself by the production of light, as in this case; the solution of a bit of marble in an acid, and the evolution of gas accompanying the solution, is a simple case in point.

We have here, then, lying altogether outside the mechanical properties of matter, so far as we know, a lot of other properties to which we give names, suppose magnetism, electricity, chemical affinity. Agreeing with one another in so far as that they do so lie, they are yet very different from one another; and, so far as we have seen at present, appear to have no connection with one another.

I have mentioned the solution of a bit of marble in acid as an instance of the action of chemical affinity. Suppose that instead of marble we have a piece of zinc, immersed, say, in dilute sulphuric acid. Like the marble, it dissolves with evolution of gas from the

surface of the metal. If we had used copper instead
of zinc, it would have remained intact, and nothing,
apparently at least, would be going on. We might
even have zinc and copper separately in the same
solution, and the result would still be the same—
the zinc would be dissolved with evolution of gas
from its surface, and the copper would remain
unaltered.

But suppose the two metals, instead of lying
apart in the same solution, were in contact at one
or more points, the phenomena now observed would
be in one respect completely changed. As before, the
zinc would be dissolved and the copper would not,
but the bubbles of gas which formerly rose from the
surface of the zinc now rise from the surface of the
copper. If, instead of being in contact within the
solution, the two metals are apart, as in the first
case, but are joined by a metallic wire, which, for
simplicity's sake, we may suppose to be wholly in
air, the metal plates jutting out above the surface
of the fluid, and the wire touching them both above
that surface, the result will be the same as in the
second of the cases mentioned above. And if the
wire, while kept in contact with one of the plates,
be sometimes held apart from the second plate and
sometimes connected with it, the result will alternately be the same as in the first, or as in the second
of the cases mentioned in the first instance.

We see, accordingly, that the result of the chemical changes which take place just alike in the two cases, so far as relates to the nature of the substances undergoing chemical change and of those produced by that chemical change, are in certain other respects quite different, in consequence of some mysterious office fulfilled by the connecting wire. The wire is not chemically changed; but that there is something going on in it is shown, not merely by the difference of result which it makes as regards the place of evolution of the gas (hydrogen) which is produced by the chemical reactions, but by other phenomena unconnected with, or, at any rate, having no apparent connection with, chemical affinity. Suppose, for example, that a magnetic needle is held near the connecting wire. So long as the wire is in contact with one only of the metallic plates no effect is produced on the needle, but as soon as contact is made between the wire and the other plate, the needle is deflected. It would lead me quite too far from my subject to mention the laws according to which this deflection takes place; this brief reference to Oersted's great discovery will suffice for my purpose. For the same reason I will leave unmentioned the great discoveries as regards the mutual relations of chemical affinity, electricity, and magnetism, which we owe to our own countryman, the illustrious Faraday. Indeed,

I cannot help thinking that it may already have occurred to the minds of some of you to ask, What can all this have to do with the proper subject of a Gifford Lecture?

In what I have been saying, I have purposely confined myself hitherto to phenomena relating to the inorganic world, because, mysterious as some of these phenomena still are—indeed, I might say, as all are, if we attempt to get to the bottom of them—we nevertheless know a good deal about them, and are able to trace to a considerable extent a chain of causation running through them. Before leaving this subject, let me briefly recapitulate the conclusions to which we have been conducted.

We have seen that the mechanical properties of matter do not suffice for the explanation of the phenomena which are presented to us. We are obliged to recognise other influences at work—influences belonging, so far as our knowledge extends, to a different platform altogether. We cannot indeed affirm, nor have we any inducement to affirm, that they are certainly inexplicable by reference to mere mechanical causes; all we can say is, we see no way of so explaining them.

Let us now pass from the contemplation of inorganic to that of organic nature. In connection with life, we see processes going on which, so far as we know, have absolutely no counterpart in the inorganic world. As in the study of inanimate nature, we found that the mechanical properties of matter did not suffice, but we were obliged to recognise other influences, such as chemical affinity, electricity, etc., lying outside those properties, so far, at least, as our knowledge can enable us to say; so it seems to me that in the study of organic nature we are obliged to recognise influences at work belonging to a different platform from the mechanical properties of matter, chemical affinity, magnetism, electricity, etc., and all the other influences belonging to the inorganic world put together.

I suppose that this would be almost universally admitted. Yet there seems to be in the minds of some a strong tendency to refer the phenomena of life, curious and complicated as they are, to the mere operation of the same forces which we observe in connection with unorganised matter. I would specially emphasise the word *mere*, for I do not for a moment want to exempt living things from the operation of the same forces to which lifeless matter is subject. But there is all the difference in the world between necessary and sufficient—between subjection to these forces and subjection to nothing else. Between the phenomena which living things exhibit, and those of lifeless matter, there appears, however, to be a great gulf fixed. Superficial resemblances may now and then be noticed, but it needs but little examination to find how purely superficial these resemblances are. Certain substances in crystallising on the side of a vessel or on the surface of a solid, on which they are deposited from a condition of vapour, not unfrequently take on fern-like forms; the ice deposited on window panes in winter is a familiar example. But with the common exhibition of graceful flowing forms all resemblance ceases. A small portion of the ice presents a perfectly homogeneous structure; there is nothing in the slightest degree analogous to the growth and multiplication of cells, let alone that marvellous power of reproduction which all living things exhibit. The ice, it is true, exhibits in polarised light the property of depolarisation, as do also various animal and vegetable structures; but this is no proof whatsoever of a similarity of origin. In fact, the property of depolarisation is referable simply to the arrangement of the ultimate molecules, of which we have strong reason for believing that ponderable matter is made up, not being, on the average, alike in all directions; and the condition of *not alike* is the general one which we should rather expect to find than not, provided there is any directing force at work interfering with the average uniform orientation of a vast number of molecules placed at random. In the case of growing crystals, we have such in the

polarities of the molecules, causing, as we have
reason to believe, a definite orientation in the individual molecules, from which results the definite
law which regulates the directions of the natural
faces and cleavage planes; in the latter it may be
that the solid particles, as they are successively laid
down in the process of growth, have a different molecular orientation, according as we regard the direction
in which a structure is being added to, or a different
direction; or it may be that, after the matter has
first been laid down in the solid state, swellings or
contractions take place in different parts of the structure which have, for effect, to introduce mechanical
strains; and we know that such strains produce a
depolarising structure, as we see exhibited in unan-
nealed glass, or glass subject to temporary bending.
Hence no valid argument for analogy of condition
between organic and inorganic material can be drawn
from the mere possession in common of the power of
depolarising polarised light.

The processes of growth and nutrition of living
things are truly wonderful, and their power of reproduction seems to be even more wonderful still.
If we are obliged to refer the former to influences
of some kind over and above those which are manifested by lifeless matter, still less could we expect to
explain the latter by the mere action of the physical
forces. But to this an objector might conceivably reply,

"I can find you an analogy in matter destitute of life," and then proceed to point out certain phenomena relating to what are called supersaturated solutions.

Sulphate of soda, otherwise called Glauber's salt, is one which, like many others, is much more soluble in hot than in cold water. If a saturated solution in hot water be made, and after boiling in a flask be allowed to cool undisturbed, the neck of the flask being protected from air, or at least from dust falling in, the salt is found to remain in solution, even though the percentage of salt be very much greater than that contained in a solution saturated with the salt in question without heating. If now the flask be opened, and the minutest fragment of the salt dropped in, it acts as a nucleus from whence crystals rapidly spread through the solution. Suppose now a number of such flasks have been prepared. On opening the first, and dropping in a minute fragment of the salt, crystallisation takes place as already described. Let now a minute quantity of the salt so formed be taken out, the second flask be opened, and the minute fragment dropped in, crystallisation now proceeds in the second flask as it did in the first, and so on indefinitely. Our imaginary objector might say : " Suppose an acorn put into the ground and left to itself; presently an oak springs up, which, in process of time, bears acorns, one of which falls on the ground, germinates, pro-

duces another oak, and so on indefinitely. Now is
not this process perfectly analogous to what has been
described as taking place with a lot of flasks containing supersaturated solutions of Glauber's salt, or,
at least, so far analogous as to warrant us in assuming that the first involves nothing more than the
action of the ordinary physical forces, seeing that
nobody supposes that anything more is involved in
the second? only in the first case, we are not able to
trace the operation of those laws; the mechanism
we have to deal with is too complicated."

I am not aware that such an argument has ever
been brought forward; the analogy is too palpably
superficial for that. Yet it is, as it seems to me,
hardly more so than the resemblance already mentioned between the forms of crystallisations and those
of growing plants.

The upshot is that, when we have life to deal
with, we must admit the existence of agencies at
work over and above those with which we are concerned when we have only lifeless matter to deal
with. We are introduced into a set of influences
belonging to a different platform altogether. And
to this platform belong, not merely the marvellous
phenomena of growth in such varied forms, both
animal and vegetable, but, more wonderful still, those
of mind, of consciousness, of will. There is something about us of which we are partly conscious, and

which we can partly control, which influences the
movements of different parts of our bodies. We
move our legs at will as in walking, and when we
are asleep the limbs remain at rest. We can, to a
limited degree, control our breathing, but it goes on
without our will or consciousness while we are asleep.
The beating of the heart goes on independently of
our will, which has no direct control over it. We
have here a graduated scale of movements more
or less voluntary. It would seem as if they were
directed by something more or less akin to will—
something at least which belongs, if I may so express
myself, to the same platform. And if there be some
such influence concerned in the movements of considerable portions of an animal frame, may it not
be to some sort of influence belonging to the same
platform that it depends that the ordinary physical
influences of chemical affinity, endosmose, etc., are
brought to bear, and directed in such a manner
that cells are formed, and living structures, whether
animal or vegetable, are built up?

The two views which may be taken of the nature
of a living organism are sharply contrasted. According to the one, that of pure materialism, a living
organism is a highly elaborate machine, constructed
out of ponderable matter, and growing and performing all the functions belonging to its life under the
influence of the physical forces and nothing more,

simply and solely by virtue of its construction. According to the other, the organism is subject indeed to all the physical forces, just like dead matter; but, over and above these, there is an influence of some kind about it, not recognisable by our senses, nor observed in relation to lifeless matter, under which the growth, and all that relates to the functions of the organism as a living thing, takes place. This influence, from its very nature, eludes our observation; we can only judge of it from its effects; it would seem, at least, according to the best conception I am able to form of it, to be something of the nature of a directing power, not counteracting the action of the physical forces, but guiding them into a determined channel.

I have spoken of this unknown mysterious influence as subject to all the physical forces, like lifeless matter. It was not always held so to be. In some of the older books we read of a supposed vital force, which was supposed to hold in check the action of chemical affinity, and so forth. I am not quite sure what was the precise idea intended to be conveyed by such statements, but it looks as if it was imagined that the vital power could actually counteract chemical affinity, etc. I think that the progress of modern science has led to an almost universal adoption of the view that there is no such counteraction, but that living things are as much subject to all the physical forces as is lifeless matter. It seems to me that this is the more philosophical view to take, and that it, at the same time, leads us to a more elevated and probably a truer view of what such an influence as that I have spoken of may possibly be akin to. It frees us from the grosser notion of antagonism, which would seem to imply that that influence was something of the nature of, or at least akin to, the physical influences which it counteracts, and leads us in our conception to place it in a higher, a more mysterious, region—a region in which we are led on to the contemplation of that mystery of mysteries, Will.

To save circumlocution, I will coin a word, and call the view which I have been endeavouring to put before you *directionism*. The alternative views would then be named materialism and directionism. In using the latter term, I do not wish you to suppose that I claim that there is anything new in an alternative to materialism, though I do not happen to have come across the precise form in which I have endeavoured to put the alternative.[1] We are familiar with the term *vital force*, which has often been used

---

[1] After the delivery of the Lecture, my attention was called to the article "Force" in Chambers's *Encyclopædia* (ed. of 1874, vol. iv. p. 421), in which the writer (Prof. Tait) has put out the same suggestion as that given above, though the trains of ideas by which we were respectively led to it would appear to have been slightly different.

by those who held that something more was required
to account for the phenomena presented by living
things than merely the forces which regulate the
condition of lifeless matter. This nomenclature does
not well accord with my ideas, because it rather sug-
gests the idea of something acting in antagonism to
the physical forces than of something which is of a
different nature altogether, and does not oppose them
but merely directs them.

But perhaps it will be said, What is the use of
speaking about what you have called directionism,
seeing that you only lead us into a region which is
so mysterious that no progress can be made? Now,
even if we assume that such is the case, it by no
means follows that the thing is useless. It is better
to fail to obtain the solution of a mathematical problem, and to be obliged to confess that we are baffled,
than to obtain a supposed solution which is false,
and which, if followed out, may lead us into further
error. In mathematics, indeed, it is usually of no
great moment; for, if we follow out a false proposition, supposing it to be true, we are usually soon
pulled up by meeting with some contradiction which
leads us to retrace our steps, so that beyond the loss
of a certain amount of time there is not much harm
done. But moral problems have not the clearness
and definiteness of mathematical ones; and if we
start with a false premiss, and reason logically upon

it, we may be led into a good deal of error without
perceiving that it is error. And the danger of
our remaining deceived is proportionate to the confidence with which we adopted the fundamental false
premiss.

But if what I have called directionism be a right
view, mysterious as is the region into which it conducts
us, progress may not perhaps be wholly impossible.
The history of the advance of physical science shows
us that progress may be made even as regards things
that, at our first acquaintance with them, seemed
to be shrouded in mystery. The pointing of a steel
needle, which had been rubbed with a lodestone, remained for centuries a mysterious fact, and yet it is
now connected with the means we use for trans-
mitting messages with practical instantaneousness to
long distances, and with the lighting of our streets
when the electric light is employed. What could
well be more mysterious than the strange ether, the
existence of which we were obliged to assume when
first it was supposed that light consisted of undulations? Yet we now know in what a marvellously
simple way the phenomena of diffraction, and other
properties of light, are explained when we adopt the
theory of undulations. I do not for a moment suppose that, even if directionism be the true view, its
adoption will lead us to similarly great discoveries
in the study of living organisms; all I mean is, that

4

the example of the physical sciences is sufficient to
forbid us to assume that the mysteriousness of the
region into which our speculations lead us authorises
us in pronouncing all progress to be impossible.

There will, I imagine, be strong reluctance felt,
especially by some of those who have devoted their
main attention to the study of natural science, to the
admission of the hypothesis of an immaterial agent,
immaterial at least in the sense of not being formed
of ponderable matter, which is capable of guiding
the action of the physical forces on the ponderable
matter of which a living organism is built up, and
which is yet not in any way recognisable by our
senses directly, nor even indirectly, by some effect
produced on something else. Of course the mere
fact of its not directly affecting our senses would not
lead any one to reject it; magnetic attraction, for
instance, does not affect our senses directly, but
we recognise its existence by its effects on bodies
external to ourselves. But the directing influence
supposed above is a thing which acts not from without but from within, and therefore, unless it were
capable of transference, we could not, so far as we
can perceive, be even indirectly informed of its presence by the action of our senses, which all involve
changes effected in the ponderable matter of our
bodies.

As bearing on the mysterious question of the relation of the mind and will to the body, I was much interested by a paper recently read by Dr. Hill, Master of Downing College, Cambridge, at a meeting of the Victoria Institute in London. It was entitled "From Reflex Action to Volition." The object of the author was not to attempt in any way to give a metaphysical theory of the action of mind and will, but simply to point out such anatomical facts that he met with in his investigations as seemed to hold out any prospect of throwing light on the above question. Naturally the minute anatomy of the brain is a matter of extreme difficulty from the soft pulpy nature of the substance, but assistance may be obtained from the employment of processes of chemical hardening, of staining, etc., such as are employed by histologists. The subject is one of which Dr. Hill has made a special study.

It has been found by physiologists that there are two kinds of nerves, called afferent and efferent, or nerves of sensation and nerves of motion, of which the office, or at least one office, is found to be, in the case of nerves of the first class, to convey sensation from the part affected to the sensorium, and that of the second to cause this or that muscle to contract. A nerve of the second kind is thrown into action, sometimes by stimulation received from a nerve of the first kind—a process which is called reflex action—

sometimes by the action of the will, the seat of which physiologists seem disposed to place in the cortex of the brain, though in this, of course, there must be a great deal of conjecture. These two kinds of stimulation may take place together in different proportions. Dr. Hill was led to the conclusion that there may be a compound path, from an afferent to an efferent nerve, resembling an electric connection by wire, provided with a shunt, one path leading through the cortex of the brain, and a shunt path not passing through it. The stimulation of the afferent nerve may thus, by being conveyed along the shunt path, give rise to a reflex action, while, at the same time, a sensation is conveyed to the mind, and the same efferent nerve may be stimulated by the action of the will; these two kinds of stimulation strengthening or opposing each other as the case may be.

It seems evident that we have here a highly complex machine, little as we can understand of its action. We seem to have a provision for giving the conscious will a certain amount of command over the motions of the parts of the body, while, at the same time, allowing motions, which may often be very important for our wellbeing, to go on without our intending them or thinking about them. But how the will commands the motions of the body, or how, conversely, external stimuli give rise to the sensations of which we are conscious, remains and must remain a mystery. Interesting as the fact is of the modes of connection which I have alluded to, wonderfully elaborate as is the machine, still that gives us no warrant for supposing that will is merely one of the modes of action of the machine, any more than we should be warranted, in consequence of the elaborate construction of an organ, in supposing that it could play a tune by virtue merely of its construction.

I have endeavoured to lay before you two alternatives between which we may make our choice. I have hitherto treated the choice as one to be made by considerations of pure philosophical probability, and I think you will have perceived in which direction my own mind leans, even when the problem is regarded as one of pure philosophy. But it is not to be concealed that the decision has an important bearing, at least so it seems to me, on questions of moral science and theology. If living things, man included, are mere machines, wonderfully constructed indeed but still only machines, mere automata, then that freedom of will of which we seem to be innately conscious, of our possession of which we seem to be as firmly convinced as we can be of anything, must be held to be only a delusion. All our actions follow inevitably from the nature and position and motions

of the ultimate molecules of our bodies at any particular moment that we take as our starting-point,
and from our environment. We are committed to
fatalism pure and simple; and how can a mere
machine be held to be responsible for what it does?

I have spoken of the mysteriousness of the region
into which the view which I have ventured to call
directionism introduces us—a region, in endeavouring to explore which we are led to the contemplation
of Will, and of the effects of its exercise. It seems
to me as if, in contemplating the phenomena of life,
we appear to be in some sense brought nearer (if in
such a subject we may speak of degrees of nearness
at all) to the Supreme Will than when we are only
considering lifeless matter, and that the increasing
mystery of the subjects of our contemplation betokens
the clouds and darkness which are round about
Him.

I have said that the logical following out of a
false premiss assumed to be true may lead us into
important error—error of a kind which may not be
easy to detect if the subjects to which it relates are
such as almost to transcend our powers of investigation. It may not be amiss to contrast, as regards
some of their influences, the adoption of the view
called materialism, and of the alternative view,
whether in the precise form to which I have given
the name "directionism," or in some allied form. In

the contrast I am about to draw, I do not profess to
do more than state what appears to my own mind
to be the tendencies of the two views respectively.
I cannot answer for the minds of others; it may be
that, in the minds of other men, the adoption of the
one view or the other may have no such tendency
as I suppose. Further, though I have spoken of
directionism, I do not see that the adoption of that
particular form of non-materialism has any particular
influence on moral or theological problems as distinguished from some other form in which the alternative to materialism may present itself to the mind;
if I feel a preference for that form, it is rather on
scientific grounds than for any consequences belonging to the domain of natural theology. But when I
say on scientific grounds, I do not, however, mean to
imply that I regard the theory as scientific, in the
sense at least of belonging to natural science, but
merely that that form of the alternative to materialism strikes me as being more nearly analogous to
what we know in science than are certain other
forms.

Perhaps one of the most salient differences, as
bearing on moral or theological questions, between
materialism and directionism, or some other non-
materialistic hypothesis, is that which relates to the
prospect of any existence for man beyond the grave.
If thought, will, consciousness are nothing more than

functions of a highly elaborate machine formed of
ponderable matter, then when that machine goes to
dissolution at death, when it is resolved, as resolved
it may be by chemical means, into its constituent
elements, it seems to me almost axiomatic, at least
to the mind of a person used to chemical contemplations, that the individual whose body has been thus
dissipated must come to an end.   Of course one may
take refuge from this conclusion in the thought that,
with God, all things are possible; one may suppose
that there will be what is tantamount to a fresh
creation altogether of a being who is a sort of ditto
of the one that perished.   But this involves such a
tremendous breach of continuity, seems so unlike all
we know of God's mode of working, as far as we can
perceive it from the study of the natural world, as
to introduce, as it seems to me, an extreme difficulty
in the way of supposing that there can be any living
existence at any time for any human being whose
body has thus been dissipated.

If, on the other hand, we suppose that there is
belonging to each individual something of the nature
of a directing power, something under which the
molecules which constitute the body are built up so
as to form its various structures, something which,
in conjunction with the material organism, brings
about the various motions of the various parts of the
body, and even the trains of thought that occupy the

mind; then as this directing power is something
distinct from and commanding ponderable matter,
something which, as it seems to me, we cannot even
on purely philosophical grounds do without, but
something at the same time, the nature of which we
cannot make out,—if, I say, we make some such
supposition as this, then we are not authorised in
affirming that this individual directing power must
come to an end at death, merely because of the complete dissipation of the ponderable matter of which
the body consisted; because of the utter breaking-up
of the elaborate machine over which this supposed
directing power was, as it were, placed in command.

Of course I do not for a moment pretend that
natural science can demonstrate, or even render
probable, such a survival. Even natural theology
can only, as I think, give dim indications of something of the kind. But I do think that natural
science can, by pointing out the insufficiency of the
materialistic hypothesis, remove the apparent incredi-
bility of any such revival, so as to leave the mind
open to weigh any evidence in favour of survival that
may come from a totally different quarter.

To pass to another point. Materialism seems to
me logically to involve fatalism, and fatalism goes
far to destroy moral responsibility. And the reason why materialism involves fatalism is, that the
materialistic hypothesis assumes that the changes

which take place in the machine, and accordingly
the train of thought itself which, according to that
hypothesis, is merely a function of the machine, take
place according to the same sort of stated inflexible
laws as those which regulate the planetary motions;
and these, as we know, can actually be made the
subject of mathematical calculation. If, on the other
hand, we recognise in life something above mere
mechanism acted on by the physical forces, we are
not conducted to fatalism, nor to the consequences
that seem to follow from it. Although I have mentioned this point of contrast, I do not suppose that
the difference between the two hypotheses is of much
practical influence in this respect; for the consciousness we possess of freedom of will, and the sense
we have of right and wrong, are too strong to be
smothered by the mere adoption of a philosophical
hypothesis.

Again, I cannot help thinking that the two modes
of contemplating living things have some tendency
towards fostering a different tone of mind. According to the materialistic view, we contemplate a
wonderful machine, the working of which, however,
we assume to lie within our means of explanation,
and which we set ourselves to explain as if it were
some complicated machine which man constructed,
though naturally there must be much about it which
we cannot hope to master. According to the other,

we feel as if we were in the presence of some
mysterious power, the nature of which transcends
our investigations, but which conducts us into a
region in which lie thought, consciousness, will. It
seems to be more conducive to a reverential tone of
mind than the other hypothesis. Of course I do
not urge this as a motive for preferring the second
alternative, for we should simply aim at the truth,
and not be led aside from it by a fancied advantage
in point of supposed beneficial effect towards the
adoption of this or that view.

LECTURE III

IF we examine the system of nature, as a whole,
from the gigantic bodies which are the object of
contemplation to the astronomer down to some
minute organism, or to some portion of the structure
of some animal which it requires the highest powers
of the microscope to reveal, we find everywhere a
scheme, the different parts of which fit into each
other in such a manner as to be conducive to the
general welfare of those organised creatures, with
respect to which alone the word "welfare" has a
definite signification. We can hardly help being
impressed with the idea that this arrangement was
designed for the objects that we see it accomplishes.
But the force with which the idea of design strikes
the mind is very different in different parts of that

vast whole; or at least I can say that so it appears to my own mind, whether rightly or wrongly I do not pretend to decide. The orderly course of the earth in its orbit round the sun is conducive to the welfare of the animals that inhabit it, man included. Shall we say that that course was designed with a view to their welfare? Perhaps, if we supposed the earth suddenly brought into being in just such a condition as we find it, we might be disposed to give an affirmative answer. But if we suppose the sun and earth formed by an evolutionary process, by the gradual condensation, according to strictly mechanical laws, along with the law of gravitation, of a portion of matter disseminated through space, in what we might regard as more or less of a haphazard way, our impression that that initial state, as we should regard it—that is to say, the state which we please to take as our starting-point in our process of evolution—was designed for the welfare of those living organisms, which, ages after, and in a very different condition of the condensed matter, might be in existence, seems at least to be a good deal weakened. And yet there is physical evidence rendering some such evolutionary process very probable.

But when, from the contemplation of these slow changes extending over vast periods of time, and taking place according to simple laws which we believe we are acquainted with, we turn to the examination in detail of some living thing, or even some one organ, the case, as it seems at least to my own mind, is very different. The impression of design then becomes so very strong that I do not see how it is to be evaded.

Instead of bringing forward a great variety of examples of the latter kind, acquaintance with which presupposes a greater knowledge of biology than I can pretend to, I propose to consider in some detail a single organ, or rather part of an organ. Let us take the eye, say the human eye; the organ adapted to that which seems, in many respects, to be the most wonderful of our senses—the sense of sight. But even with respect to this I will pass very lightly over a considerable part—that which relates to the formation of images of external objects on the retina. The means whereby this is effected, namely, through a transparent structure, having a general resemblance to the lenses, or combinations of lenses, made by the optician, and discharging its functions in a similar way, and according to the same laws—these, I say, are so generally known, and described in such elementary treatises, that I will not weary you by dwelling on them. Besides, in my former course I touched briefly on this trite subject. I will pass on then to what, in a functional sense, lies beyond the formation of images of external objects on the retina, though here we begin to enter on a mysterious

region where optics fail us, and we must endeavour
to thread our way, as best may be, by a difficult
anatomical and microscopical examination of the
structures, with the aid of such physiological knowledge which we possess as may seem to bear on the
question.

The road on which we are now entering is one
which leads us towards that great mystery, the
mental perception of the effect of stimulation of our
organs of sensation. We cannot expect to follow
the road till the goal is reached, but it is conceivable
that something may be traceable of the earlier portion of the track.

To guide us in our search after the means whereby
the end to be attained is brought about, it may be
well, in the first instance, to refer to the actual
sensations, the means for bringing which about we
are attempting in some measure to follow. For the
present I will dismiss all consideration of colour, and
regard light merely as such. Of course something
beyond this would be necessary for the perception of
colour, but of this we know very little.

Dismissing then the consideration of colour, and
attending for the present to a single eye only, let us
consider what is necessary in order to provide for
the sensations which we experience.

The eye, in its function of simply an optical
instrument, forms an image of external objects on

the retina when vision is distinct. An optical image
is made up of the separate images of all the separate
points of which we may regard the object as consisting. Each small portion of the object, of a
breadth comparable with the length of a wave of
light—comparable, that is, with the $\frac{1}{50000}$ part of an
inch—forms its image quite independently of each
other such point, and the question is, What is it that
appears to be necessary for the perception of the
image in its form, and as regards the relative
brightness of its different parts ?

If the object be a single point, the sensation is
that of a point in the field of view. If, while the eye
is perfectly steady, this point be moved to the right,
or left, or upwards, or downwards, the sensation is
that of a point in the field of view to the right or
left of, or above or below, its previous position. If
the object consists of a number of points, not too
close together, the sensation is that of a corresponding number of distinct points, the order of
sequence of which, as regards each of the two
elements of lateral displacement, is the same as that
of the objects themselves. It is found that the
smallest distance apart at which two small objects
can be placed so as still to be seen as two, is such as
to subtend at the eye an angle of about one minute,
which is about the angle subtended by a shilling at
the distance of ninety yards. The corresponding

distance of the images on the retina is about
$\frac{4}{1000}$ of a millimetre, or say the $\frac{1}{8000}$ part of an
inch. The retina must accordingly be studded in
some way with points set at this excessive closeness,
at which stimulation by light produces distinct
sensations. Nor is the portion of the retina for
which separate sensations must thus be provided by
any means small; our field of view takes in a large
angle, and the retinal structure, which will presently
be mentioned, and which unquestionably appears to
be that on which this vast multiplicity of separate
sensations depends, extends over a portion of the
back of the eye exceeding a hemisphere.

Imagine a hollow hemisphere with a radius of
ninety yards, and having the eye in its centre, to be
lined with shillings set as close as possible to one
another, and the number of shillings will represent
in a general way the number of separate sensations
that have to be provided for, or at least that would
have to be provided for if the acuteness of vision
were everywhere as great as in the middle of the
field.

The sense of sight is confined to a portion of the
back of the eyeball; that of touch extends all over
the body. It cannot be doubted that it is in some
way by means of the nerves, running as they do from
all parts of the body to the brain, or rather of one
class of these nerves, that the sensation of touching

5

something with such or such a part of the body is conveyed to the mind. If the sensory nerves supplying a limb be cut across, there is a loss of sensation in the limb. Now when the retina is examined, it is found to be very richly supplied with nerve fibres. These form a plexus on the inner side of the retina, the side towards the centre of the ball, and ultimately unite into one large bundle, forming the optic nerve, which runs out of the eyeball, not in the axis of vision, but a little to one side of it, towards the nose. It then continues its course through the optic commissure into the brain.

That the office of these nerves relates to vision is shown, among other things, by the fact that in cases in which it is necessary to remove an eye, when the surgeon comes to the cutting across of the optic nerve, the sensation of the patient is not that of pain, but of a flash of light.

When the nerve filaments are followed in the opposite direction, it is found that they begin to turn outwards into the less deeply situated portions of the retina. Careful dissection and microscopic examination show that the retina consists of several layers, nearly the last of which, the so-called "bacillary layer," is a very remarkable structure.

This layer is composed of a vast number of closely set, elongated bodies, pointing outwards from the centre of the eyeball, and accordingly in the

middle of the eyeball backwards. They are of two
forms, some, called *rods*, being cylindrical; others,
called *cones*, tapering outwards. The latter are
shaped much like slender peg-tops, with the broader
ends turned towards the light. In the human eye,
in the very middle of the retina, where vision is
most acute, there are cones only, the points of which
are arranged very much like the seeds in a head of
the large sunflower. On proceeding a very little
distance laterally, from the middle of the retina, the
cones are separated from one another by the rods in
single layer; and a little further still, and from
thence onwards till near the end of the bacillary
layer, the cones are further apart, so as to be
separated by more than one layer of rods; and
accordingly the rods, being slenderer than the
thicker part of the cones, are much more numerous
than the cones. The outer extremities of the rods
reach to a thin layer which contains the black
pigment, and from which filaments containing grains
of pigment come down and lie between the rods.
The outer extremities of the cones do not reach quite
so far; but under the stimulus of light the filaments
above mentioned come down, so as to lie between
the outer segments of the cones as well as of the
rods. From the inner extremities of both rods and
cones are seen excessively delicate nerve fibres
running at first inwards, that is, towards the centre

of the eyeball. There is every reason to believe that
they are continuous with the fibres, lying slightly
further inside, and running transversely to the
radius, which form the plexus that has been already
mentioned ; and they have been traced a great part
of the way, though not quite the whole, as there is
one narrow layer in which they get lost, so that
hitherto it has not been found possible to trace them.
These bodies, the rods and cones, provided as they
are with independent nerve fibres, are so closely
set that the distance between adjacent cones in
the middle of the retina is only about $\frac{4}{1000}$ of a
millimetre, corresponding, as we have seen, to the
calculated distance apart on the retina of the images
of two points which can only just be seen as two.
In the bacillary layer then, and there alone in
the retina, we meet with a structure furnishing
independent elements sufficiently numerous and
closely set to meet the demand for independent
sensations of the vast number of closely set points
in the field of view, which can nevertheless be seen
as independent of one another.   Accordingly these
bodies are universally regarded as the seat of perception of light, that is, the place where the stimulus
of light is applied to the nerve fibres, to be by them
conveyed, in some manner which we do not understand, to the sensorium.   It is, however, in accordance
with what we know to suppose that the stimulation

of a given nerve fibre produces a given sensation, irrespective of the position the nerve may take in consequence of the motion of parts of the body. Thus when we look at a moving point, and without moving the head keep it in the axis of vision by rotating the eyeball, the sensation is that of a point in the centre of the field of view, the same point of the retina always receiving the stimulus from the moving object, though the position of the point stimulated keeps changing relatively to the socket of the eye.

When we take a series of points in an object (which for simplicity we may suppose projected on a sphere having the eye for its centre) which lie in any order of sequence, we must get, according to the laws of optics, a series of images on the retina lying in a corresponding order of sequence; in fact, the image on the retina must be geometrically similar to the object. Experience shows that we have the sensation of a series of points lying in order of sequence like those of the object, though how this is effected we cannot tell. Were that all, the sensation would not necessarily be that of an object similar (in a geometrical sense) to the actual object; the object might be seen distorted. We find, however, that our sensations give us the idea of an object geometrically similar to the actual object, or nearly so. That the similarity is not complete, even in the

normal condition of the eye, is shown by the necessity
of a precaution with which type-founders, or rather
those who sink for them the matrices in which the
types are cast, are familiar. If the letter s or the
figure 8 be looked at in a printed page, and again
after the book has been turned upside down, the
under half will appear smaller than the upper. In
order that the letter or figure should appear to have
its upper and under halves of the same size or nearly
so, it is necessary to make the under half really a
little larger than the upper. And if the eye be in
an abnormal condition—suppose, for example, from
the effect of a slight effusion on the retina—the
deviation of the sensation from an actual representa-
tion of the object may be more pronounced; thus,
for example, a straight line may appear crooked,
and, of course, a suitably crooked line, when the
axis of the eye is directed to a definite point in it,
may appear straight. These facts seem to me to
show that our judgment of the form of an object is
not merely a matter of experience in the interpretation of our sensations, but is founded on our sensations themselves. It seems probable that it has
to do with the way in which the nerve fibres are
distributed in the brain, whereas the stimulation
depends on the way in which the percipient organs
are distributed in the retina, since it is on that that
it depends what particular elements it shall be that

receive a stimulus from such or such a point of the image. Hence, given the distribution in the brain (or whatever else it may be that determines the order of lateral succession of the sensation of points in the field of view), a correlative distribution is demanded in the retinal ends of the nerve fibres, in order that the sensation of form may correspond, at least very approximately, to the reality.

To show this more clearly, imagine the object to be a series of concentric circles, to the centre of which the eye is directed. Then the image on the retina will also be a series of concentric circles, and experience shows that we have the sensation of a series of concentric circles. Imagine now that the rods and cones were altered in position on the retina without altering their respective connections with the sensorium. Suppose, for example, that the alteration of position was such that, without any alteration in the order of sequence, the concentric rings of percipient organs, on which fell the images of the rings in the object, were so altered in position as to form a series of concentric squares. By hypothesis the sensation would remain the same as before, provided the same elements received the same stimulation as before. But in order that the stimulation should be the same as before, the image of the stimulating object must now be a series of concentric squares; and as the object and image

must be similar, the object must itself be a series
of concentric squares. Hence, on the supposed
distribution of the percipient organs, an object
consisting of a series of concentric squares, to the
centre of which the eye was directed, would be seen
as a series of concentric circles. And by making
other suppositions as to the mode of alteration of
the positions of the percipient elements in the
retina, all sorts of outlandish transformations would
ensue. It is a curious subject for speculation how
far the clearness of our geometrical ideas might have
been affected if there had been from birth upwards
this want of correspondence between our sensations of form and the actual forms of the objects
looked at.

Hitherto I have spoken of one eye only. The two
eyes perform similar functions, and yet we have a
single sensation produced by them. How is this?
Let us take a single visible point in the first instance.
If we view it first with the right eye and then with
the left eye, we have in each case the sensation of a
single point. If we use both eyes together, and the
axes of the eyes are casually directed, then we see
two points, one with each eye. But if we direct the
axes of both eyes towards the point, as we habitually
do when we have a single point to look at, then
instead of the sensation of two points we have that of

but one. The two sensations blend into one, so far
at least as position in the field is concerned. This
shows that the two points on the retina, in which it
is cut by the visual axes, correspond in such a manner
that, when the nerves there ending are stimulated,
we have the sensation of a single point in the field
of view. Nor is this unity of sensation by any means
confined to the particular pair of points in which the
retinas of the two eyes are cut by the axes of vision.
If, while we direct our eyes to one particular point,
other points in the object are noticed which lie a
little to the right or left of or above or below the
point first mentioned, to which the axes of the eyes
are kept steadily directed, it will be found that these
other points like the first are seen single, though all
the points can be seen double in a moment by directing the axes of the eyes as if towards an object considerably nearer. This shows that there are a vast
number of pairs, and not merely a single pair, of
"corresponding" points in the retinas of the two
eyes, corresponding in the sense that if both points
of the pair are simultaneously stimulated, the sensation is that of a single point, and not of two points,
in the field of view. And the following two questions
present themselves to us to be answered if we can:—
(1) How is it that the sensation of a single point in
the field of view is produced when two points, lying
in the retinas of the two eyes respectively, are simul-

taneously stimulated, provided the two points are corresponding points ? (2) How is it that if one point in the object, which I will suppose to be some way off, is seen single, so that its images in the two eyes are situated at corresponding points, the images of the other points of the object, or at least of such as are situated at no very great angular distance from the first, also fall on corresponding points ? I say, "or at least of such as are situated at no very great angular distance from the first," because, when we recede to a considerable distance from the centre of the field of vision, when we look, as it is said, "with the corner of the eye," our estimation of the position of an object becomes less and less sharp, and we can less accurately judge whether or no the images seen with the two eyes respectively appear strictly coincident.

The first question is one which is involved in the great mystery of our sensations. Yet the nerves, which appear to form the link of connection between the percipient organ and the mental sensation, are visible objects, and by following their course so far as it can be followed, we might conceivably obtain some hint as to a provision for unity of sensation in spite of duplicity of perception. Now in each eye the retinal nerve fibres are collected into a single bundle, forming the optic nerve, which runs out of the eyeball, not in the place where the retina is cut by the axis of the eye, but to one side of it, towards the nose, and not quite, though nearly, on the same level. Now, as I have already said, the two optic nerves, in their course into the brain, run together into the " optic commissure," from whence run two nerve trunks, consisting of bundles of nerve fibres, into the " optic tracts " in the right and left halves of the brain.   It seems tempting to suppose that some sort of connection might take place in the commissure between nerve fibres belonging to corresponding points on the retinas of the two eyes which might bring about unity of sensation.   But as some very rare cases are on record, in which dissection after death showed that the optic nerve from each eye ran separately to the optic tract on the same side of the brain, and yet no peculiarity of vision is recorded as having been noticed during life, it would seem as if the union of the two nerves in the optic commissure were at least not essential.   So all we can do is to classify the phenomenon with other instances of duplication of perception; for example, we judge the pitch of a musical note to be the same, whether we hear it with the right ear or with the left.

The second question, like the first, involves the mysterious subject of our sensations, but it also involves the distribution of visible objects—the rods and cones—in the retinas of the two eyes.   In the latter respect it is more amenable to our investigation of

what it is that is demanded, in order that the object
to be accomplished may actually be attained. Now,
according to what I have been arguing, if we suppose
the nerve fibres coming from the various points of
the retina of, say, the right eye to be labelled according to the position in the field of view of the points
of which they would, if stimulated, respectively give
us the sensation, there must be a corresponding
arrangement, geometrically similar, or nearly so, in
the distribution of the distal ends of the nerve fibres,
and accordingly in the rods or cones to which they
lead in the retina. And in order that the two eyes
should correspond throughout, this distribution must
be the same, or very nearly so, in the two retinas;
and not only must they be the same in the two eyes
thought of as loose and independent, but further,
when the eyes come to be directed on an object, their
positions in their sockets must be such that the images
of the object shall fall on corresponding points in the
two eyes. What this requires may be understood by
a simple illustration. Imagine two sheets of paper
laid one on the other, and in that position pricked
through with a pin in a number of points. Let the
sheets now be separated; let one remain fixed; let the
other be placed in the same plane as the first, but
otherwise at random; and consider what motions must
be given to the second to make the pin-holes in the
two fit. We must clearly provide for two motions of

translation, in different directions, and also for a
motion of rotation. And, of course, if we want the
pin-holes to fit, it is indifferent whether one sheet only
be moved or else both. Both may be provided with
means of making independently the three motions.
Now suppose the eyes directed to any object. Let
any group of points in the object be selected for consideration. This group will furnish two images on
the two retinas respectively, each consisting of a
group of points, the same in every respect for the
two, as I am not now considering the small difference on which stereoscopic vision depends. The
image of the points on one, say the right, retina
will form a group of points falling on a group of
percipient elements. To each of these there will
be a corresponding element in the left retina,
and this group will, by the first demand, agree in
size and pattern with the group of corresponding
elements in the right eye, and therefore with the
image which falls on them, and therefore with the
image in the left eye, as the two images are just
alike. But though the group of percipient elements
in the left eye agrees in size and pattern with the
group of images in the same eye, the two groups may
not be coincident, but may be like the pin-holes on
the sheets of paper in our illustration after one of
the sheets had been disturbed from the position it
occupied when the holes were pricked. If this be

so, the images in the two eyes will fall on non-corresponding points, and the person will see two images of the object in the field of view, one being seen by the right eye and the other by the left. These, however, can be brought into coincidence by properly rotating the left eye, if there be means provided for so doing. Now each eyeball is provided with one pair of muscles, by which it can be rotated about a vertical axis; with another pair, by which it can be rotated about a horizontal axis running right and left; and with a third pair, running in a direction oblique to the axis, by which it can be rotated about the line of sight. Here, then, we have a provision, by means of which the eyeballs can be adjusted for single vision, and we habitually so adjust them. The three pairs of muscles are not, however, called into use to the same extent in the habitual employment of the eyes. The pair for rotation round a vertical axis are in constant requisition as we direct the eyes to the right or left; and, moreover, we are constantly rotating the two eyeballs differently, in adjusting the eyes for single vision of near or distant objects. The pair for rotation about a horizontal axis running right and left are also in constant requisition for looking upwards or downwards; but in this motion we do not require to rotate the eyeballs unequally. Lastly, as regards rotation of the eyeballs round their own axes, this is a motion which we are not

called on to perform at all; as regards orientation
in this respect, if the eyeballs were set in the right
position, they would remain right, provided they did
not rotate round their own axes.

What, then, it might perhaps be asked, is the use
of our being furnished with oblique muscles at all?
And as regards rotation round a horizontal axis
running right and left, what is the advantage, if there
be any, in having muscles for the independent rotation of the two eyeballs, seeing that, in the use of the
eyes, they are always called on to rotate together
through equal angles?

Now if the eyes were exactly in adjustment one
with another as regards rotation round a right and
left horizontal axis, so that when the eyes were
directed straight forwards, the points of the retinas
in the axes of vision should be at the same level; and
if the rotations about a right and left horizontal axis
were always the same for the two eyes; and if,
again, the eyeballs were so placed in their sockets
that, if a line were drawn horizontally in the retina
of one eye through the point in which it is cut by
the axis of vision, the locus of the percipient elements
in the other retina which correspond respectively
with those which, in the first, lay in the drawn line,
should also form a horizontal line; and if, furthermore, the visual sensation which we experience, in
consequence of the excitement of these elements by

the necessarily horizontal image of a horizontal line, were at least approximately that of a horizontal line, not, for example, that of a line inclined at 45° to the horizon—if, as I say, all these conditions were fulfilled, then indeed the two eyes might perform their function of giving single vision. But a slight deviation from the exact fulfilment of either of the first two conditions which we have been supposing stereotyped would be fatal, and would lead to the great inconvenience and confusion arising from double vision, unless we were to keep one of our eyes closed, using, it may be, sometimes the one and sometimes the other, but not both together. And how is the necessary accuracy of relative position to be effected in a structure which, like the rest of the body, has to grow from small beginnings? or if effected for one position of the eyeballs, how is it to be maintained, seeing that the eyeballs have to move so freely in their sockets?

These desiderata are satisfied by providing that the proper relative position of the eyeballs shall be maintained, not in an invariable manner, but by means of muscles under the control, at least to a certain extent, of the will. That we have such a power of adjustment, even as regards those motions which we are not habitually called on to perform, may be shown by very simple experiments. To show that we can adjust relatively to each other the positions of the two eyeballs with regard to a horizontal axis running right and left, we have only to look through spectacles at a printed page, and then turn the spectacles very slightly round an axis passing forwards through the bridge. At first the letters are seen double, one image being over the other, not side by side, as when we look towards an object, but direct the axes of vision towards a point nearer or further off than the object. But if the spectacles were not turned too much, on continuing to gaze the two images blend into one. In the endeavour to see single, the will almost unconsciously directs the muscles so as to rotate the eyeballs into the position demanded. By a somewhat similar, though less simple experiment, it may be shown that we have a power of adjustment as regards rotation of the eyeballs, or one of them, about an axis pointing forwards. By the six muscles with which each eyeball is provided we are enabled, not merely to direct the axes of vision of the two eyes towards any desired point, but to secure the relative adjustments requisite for single vision. And in making the necessary effort we appear to be guided by an almost unconscious desire to see single.

I have spoken as if the oblique muscles rotated the eyeball about an axis running directly forward. Their direction is such as to give rise to the suspicion that they might rotate the eyeball about a line

6

inclined at a considerable angle to a line pointing
directly forwards. I am disposed, however, to think
that this is not the case. The only small rotation
which could be given to the eyeball by the oblique
muscles, without altering the length of the straight
muscles, is one about an axis pointing forwards; and
if the direction of the pull made by one of the
oblique muscles be not in the equatorial plane of
the eye (as we may call a plane drawn perpendicular
to a line drawn straight forwards), it by no means
follows that the rotation produced will be about an
axis considerably inclined to the axis of vision. In
fact, the pull, even if supposed oblique, is equivalent
to one perpendicular to, and one parallel to, the axis
of vision. The former would produce a rotation
about the axis of vision, and rotation from the latter
would be prevented by the straight muscles. It is
noteworthy that the attachment of the oblique
muscles to the eyeball lies in the equatorial plane,
the only position in which a small rotation, given by
any of the straight muscles, would displace the points
of attachment of the oblique muscles in a direction
perpendicular to that in which they are displaced
when they do their own work. Thus provision
appears to be made for the *independent* action of
each pair of muscles in giving a rotation about one
or other of three rectangular axes.

The theory that we are, in fact, guided in rotating

our eyeballs by the desire of seeing singly, however
long-continued habit may render us unconscious that
we are exercising any guidance at all, is confirmed
in a striking manner by the known possibility of
curing in certain cases the defect of squinting without having recourse to an operation. A friend of
mine, in consequence of having been thrown from a
vehicle, had the direction of the axis of one of his
eyes thrown out of adjustment by as much as 18° or
thereabouts, and was no more able to set it right
than an ordinary person would be to set his wrong
to a similar extent. The ophthalmic surgeon whom
he consulted effected a complete cure by prescribing
the use of prismatic spectacles. To start with, a
pair was employed in which, in lieu of a lens, a prism
was placed opposite to the defective eye of such kind
as to produce a deviation which nearly, but not quite,
brought the images seen by means of the affected
eye into coincidence with those seen with the normal
eye. A slight angular movement of the eyeball,
which the patient was capable of making, then
sufficed to bring the images seen by means of the
two eyes into coincidence. When these spectacles
had been habitually worn for some time, the adjustment to this extent was made without conscious
effort, and then the spectacles were changed for a
pair with a prism of lower power, and so on by small
steps at a time till the cure was complete.

The wonderful structure of the human eye, and
its adaptation to the functions of the organ, naturally
give rise to reflections bearing on the object of the
Gifford Foundation. I will not, however, further
occupy your time to-day, but will leave this part of
the subject to the commencement of my next Lecture.

LECTURE IV

Evidence of design afforded by the minute structure of the retina
—Analogy of the muscles that rotate the eyeball to adjusting
screws—Evidence of provision for the welfare of the creature
—Whether the benefits resulting from gravitation can be
adduced as evidence of the same—Sensation of colour—
Evidence of provision for enjoyment—Discussion of the
validity of the argument.

In my last Lecture I endeavoured to bring before
you some of the results arrived at by the dissection
and microscopical examination of the human eye,
combined with such light as may be shed by our
optical knowledge on its functions in relation to
its minute structure. That the minute percipient
organs, the number of which in each eye must be
reckoned by millions, and which require to be so
accurately arranged relatively to one another, not to
speak of their relation to the sensations produced—
that these, I say, could have come into existence as
an accumulated result of mere haphazard variations
without direct design, seems to my own mind
incredible. Nor can I help referring to the analogy
which the mechanism for effecting the adjustment of

the eyes to single vision presents to the work of man. The astronomer requires, for the prosecution of his science, telescopes mounted in particular ways, to allow him to observe the heavenly bodies with the accuracy which modern science requires. He may require, for instance, to have a telescope mounted so as to turn round an axis which is strictly horizontal, and which is set in a direction perpendicular to the plane of the meridian, or to have it mounted so as to move in some other way no less definite. And in instruments of precision generally, it constantly happens that they are required to have, very accurately, certain movements which cannot be ensured with the requisite exactness in the construction of the strong parts of the instrument. In such cases the constructor of the instrument takes care that the strong parts shall be so made that the instrument shall move very approximately in the manner demanded, and he provides it with screws or other means of adjustment, by means of which the observer may make the fulfilment of the required movements practically complete.

Now in the maintenance of single vision, notwithstanding the multitude of angular motions which the eyeballs are constantly making as we look from object to object, right or left, up or down, close at hand, or a good way off, we notice a plan of very

similar character. The requisite accuracy of adjustment is provided for by means of six muscles for
each eyeball, which are under the control of the
will, by means of which the requisite adjustments
can be, and are, effected. The requisite adjustments
become so habitual that we are unconscious of
making them, and it is not easy to learn how to
make unnatural movements of the eyeballs, that is
to say, movements different from those which we are
constantly making in the normal use of our eyes.
These muscles take the place of the adjusting screws
in the illustration which I have ventured to give;
but, whereas in actual instruments the adjustments
are troublesome, and are made only occasionally, in
the use of our eyes we are making them almost at
every moment; for while we are awake our eyeballs
are constantly moving about.

Taking the organ as a whole, it seems to me, as I
have already said, that the evidence of design in the
construction is overwhelming. But when I say this,
I by no means mean to maintain that each element
of the structure must be regarded as formed expressly
and independently. The operation of what are
called second causes is by no means excluded. Only
we know so very little about the operation of causes
of this nature as regards the structure of living
things, that if such there be, we are unable to follow
it. And if there be any truth in the speculation

which I ventured to bring before you, of the operation in things endowed with life of something of the nature of a directing power, it does not seem likely that we shall ever be able to get much further; least of all, if we insist on rejecting everything which lies beyond the laws at which we have arrived, or may yet arrive, in the investigation of the properties and phenomena of matter which is not endowed with life.

Admitting the validity of the argument for design which the study of the eye affords, we cannot fail to be struck with the provision which has been made, even in minute details, for the welfare of the creature. Instances of similar benevolent provision might indeed be brought forward in great number, but, as I said already, I preferred to take some one instance and dwell on it at some length. I have chosen the eye, partly because my own studies have led me to pay special attention to it, and as I cannot pretend to be a biologist, I thought it safest to select that organ which I fancied I knew best; partly because it seems pre-eminently to afford an example of a specially refined and complicated construction, the object of which, taken as evidenced by its functions, we are able to a considerable degree to explain. And the reason why we are specially struck with the evidence of design by the study of the eye seems to me to be this : that we are shut

in to the contemplation of a subject of limited extent,
such as our minds can grasp. So far as we know,
the arrangement, for instance, of the percipient
organs in the retina might have been quite different—
might have been such as grievously to interfere with
the use of the organ; and yet we are not acquainted
with any general law obliging them, so to speak, to be
what they actually are. Did we know of such a
law, the argument for design would have been
shifted from a consideration of the immediate
construction to that of the establishment of the law
in question; and as a general law of such a kind as
we have been supposing would have had a great
variety of consequences, of which we are supposed to
know, or at any rate to have under our contemplation, only this one, we should not, I think, feel the
same sort of confidence that the law was designed for
this particular result. Indeed, it might even seem
presumptuous to say that it was, seeing what a
multitude of consequences such a law must have—
consequences the utility of which we are not able to
take a comprehensive view of, so as to estimate their
advantage.

By way of contrast I will now take a general law
with which we are well acquainted, and point out
one way in which we derive advantage from it.

The planets circulate round the sun, and one at

least of those planets—the earth on which we live, regarded as one of a brotherhood of planets—is a suitable habitation for man and animals of various kinds. If at any particular moment we were to imagine the planets to occupy their actual positions, and to be moving with their actual velocities, and were then to inquire what, according to the laws of motion, would become of them, supposing them all independent of one another and of the sun, we know that they would not go on circulating round the sun as they do, but would move away altogether into space, pursuing straight courses, and moving each with a uniform velocity. Supposing even that at starting they were furnished with plants and animals, they would soon get so far away from the sun that the light and heat received from it would become utterly insignificant, and all living things, be they plants or animals, would perish; our own earth, in which water so largely abounds, would, in a large part of it, become coated with a solid crust of ice, one or two or three miles in thickness. To prevent such a result a force must act, continually drawing the planets downwards towards the sun from the tangents to their paths, which they continually tend to move in by virtue of the laws of motion. Such a force is secured by a property of matter whereby any two portions attract each other with a force depending on the distance.

But it is not sufficient that the planets should be
drawn towards the sun from the rectilinear paths
which they continually tend to follow. That might
be the case, and yet the orbits might be unstable,
and a planet, even if it moved for a time in an orbit
not very greatly differing from a circle with the sun
near the centre, might yet, in the long run, by virtue
of the disturbances consequent on the attraction of
the planets for one another, get so near the sun as
to be scorched, or move away so far as to be frozen
up. Now it has been shown by mathematicians that
if the mutual attraction between two bodies follows
the law which Newton, the discoverer of the law of
gravitation, proved that universal gravitation does
follow; then if at one time the planets were moving
in orbits only moderately eccentric, and in planes
not greatly inclined to one another, that feature of
the orbits would be permanent, notwithstanding the
slow secular changes which the orbits might undergo
in consequence of the perturbations of the planets
by one another. A consequence would be that the
habitable condition of the planets, or of such of them
as were habitable, would be maintained.

The question now arises, Have we a right to
regard the property of gravitation as designedly
impressed upon matter, in order that the planets
might be suited for habitations to living things, in

the same way as we had been led to regard the
arrangement of the percipient organs (given that
such organs exist) in the retina, as designed to bring
about a correspondence of sensation with the object
seen, and singleness of vision with the two eyes?
Ought the inference of design to be equally strong
in the two cases, and accordingly valid in the one
case if valid in the other, invalid in the one case if
invalid in the other, or is there a difference between
the circumstances in the two cases of such a nature
as to justify the feeling a difference in the strength
of the argument?

Now in the second case (that of gravitation) we
are dealing with a general law which must have a
vast number of consequences, many of them bearing
in a very material manner on our welfare. By
hypothesis we have in contemplation only one very
special consequence, and we cannot say the law was
necessary even to bring about that. The problem of
determining whether or no the orbits would retain
that character of rough circularity in spite of
perturbations, supposing the attracting force to
vary as any arbitrary function of the distance, so
as to enable us to say whether other laws than that
which we know gravitation to follow would equally
succeed in retaining a suitability of character in
the orbits—this problem, I say, has not, so far as I
know, been attacked. It would probably be one of

very considerable difficulty, and there are only the
slenderest motives for engaging in those difficulties.
So that, as regards the proposed question concerning
design, we are not even able to say that it is not
merely sufficient but necessary that the law of
attraction should be what it is. When I speak of
the necessity as doubtful, or at least as not having
(so far as I know) been fully investigated, I do not of
course ignore what is well known to mathematicians
—that a law according to the direct distance would
entail perfect stability, and unchangeableness of
orbits. But the proposal of such a law for
actual attraction would only be of the nature of
a mathematical conundrum, since it would make
the effect of one body in modifying the motion of
another greater and greater, without any limit, if we
suppose it *further* and further off.

Where we have a general law, such as the law of
gravitation, entailing a host of consequences, and we
single out one particular beneficial consequence, it
seems to me hardly reverent to ask the question
whether we may regard the law as designedly laid
down, in order to bring about that particular
consequence. The existence of the law affects the
whole system of nature, and it is utterly beyond us
to say how that system, as a whole, might have been
altered had the law been different from what it is.
In such a case, it seems to me that we should rather

take the system of nature as a whole, and the laws
of nature, so far as we have been able to discover
them as a whole, and consider how the whole fits
together in such a manner as to be conducive to
our welfare. I think a too minute dissection of the
processes of nature, with a view to bring out evidences
of design, should rather be held in check by a due
feeling of reverence, and that the free indulgence of
it may tend to make our ideas of the Author of
nature too anthropomorphic.

On the whole, then, I think that there are legitimate
differences in the applicability of beneficial results to
the argument for design, or at least in the mode of
their application. In some cases the evidence of
design seems to be so palpable that he may run
who reads. In other cases, if we attempt to trace
design in some beneficial result, we are led to the
contemplation of laws so teeming with consequences
that we feel ourselves quite unable to estimate them
as a whole. Thus, on the one hand, we are taught
that we are not to merge our ideas of God in that of
a system of general laws, keeping out of sight the
idea of personality (in the sense in which, in my
former course, I endeavoured to explain the term
as applied to God), and virtually denying to Him
the power of will, of intention, of which we are
innately conscious in ourselves; while, on the other
hand, we are reminded that God is not subject to

human limitations, nor is His way of working like. man's way of working.

In bringing forward the structure of animals, and more especially man, as evincing design, I have hitherto confined myself to a single one of our organs of sense. But the structure of the bodies of men and animals evinces, I may say at every turn, evidence of what, to say the least, *appears* to be the result of design. If, as regards one organ, which has the appearance of being in some respects the most refined and elaborate of the whole, or at least of those, the functions of which we are in any way enabled to explain, the evidence of design is so over-whelming that we are compelled to admit it, then we are forbidden by logical consistency to put out of court the idea of design in considering the origin of other parts of the structure. I do not for a moment say that we are in any way debarred from endeavouring to co-ordinate the observed phenomena regarding the structure—from endeavouring to refer them to the operation of general laws. Such is the character of progress in science. But it is one thing to endeavour to make progress in this direction—to suppose that further progress is possible, and even likely to be obtained—and quite a different thing to assume that this is all that we require; that if our progress were sufficient no room would be left for the idea of design ; or at least that, if any were left, the evidence would be wholly of a different nature, that arising from the mutual adaptations of the different parts of a vast whole, which itself is the necessary outcome of a few fundamental laws, laws as simple in their way as the laws of motion.

It would, I think, be a very useless expenditure of time and thought to speculate as to how our ideas of natural theology would be affected if we were able to explain the whole system of nature, organic and inorganic just alike, as we now explain by the laws of motion the movement of a rigid body left to itself. We have quite enough to do, more than enough to take up our whole attention, in endeavouring to investigate the conditions of the world in which we actually live, without transporting ourselves in imagination into a fairy world, in which we fancied ourselves so to have got to the bottom of everything, that it should appear as if it were inconceivable that things could have been other than what they are. Far as our investigations may extend, the region of what we know is surrounded by a region of which we are ignorant. It is as if on a perfectly dark night we used artificial light to allow us to explore the objects about us. By increasing the power of our light we continually add fresh objects, which previously lay in darkness, to those of which we are able to make out the forms; but at the same time we continually widen the circle of

darkness which surrounds the objects that we have
been able to make out.

The wonderful sense of sight, even if we regard it
as restricted to enabling us to perceive the forms of
external objects, is obviously of the highest importance to our material wellbeing. But besides this,
it continually affords us pleasure, as we admire the
graceful forms of plants or animals, or the elegant
markings which they so frequently exhibit; or, again,
as we contemplate the rugged mountain, or the
ocean, at one time smooth and tranquil, at another
time agitated by waves which travel along the surface and dash against the rocks, giving, when seen
from no great distance, a grand idea of their mechanical power. But this sense does more than merely
enable us to perceive the forms of external objects,
and the varieties of light and shade which their sur-
faces exhibit. We have, besides all this, the sensation of a variety of colours, adding immensely to the
beauty of the objects which present themselves to
our vision. As regards the perception of form, we
have seen that the structure of the eye gave some
slight insight of the way in which it is brought
about; not of course that we have any idea of the
way in which our bodily organs act upon our minds,
but merely that we find some indications of a
mechanism that appears to be destined to afford
communication between the part which the light

reaches before it ceases to exist as light and the
sensorium, which we have reason to believe is situated in the brain.   But as regards the perception
of colour, we are not at present able to go even so
far as this, though it is quite conceivable that further
research may some day reveal a structure that
appears destined to convey messages, as it were,
regarding colour from the place where light first
acts on the bodily organ to the sensorium.   In consequence, however, of our present ignorance, we have
not, as it seems to me, quite as much evidence of
design regarding the perception of colour, as we have
regarding the perception of form and lighter or
darker shade; or, perhaps I should rather say, the
kind of evidence is different in the two cases.   But
the two kinds of perception—that of form and that
of colour—are so nearly allied, that we can hardly
refuse to entertain the idea of design in the latter
case when the evidence for it is so exceedingly strong
in the former.

Now from a merely utilitarian point of view—I
mean as regards material wellbeing apart from the
pleasure we may derive from the exercise of our senses
—there is a considerable difference between the two
kinds of perception.   If we saw everything in mono-
chrome, like a photograph, we might still get on very
well as regards our ordinary lives.   Modes of signal-
ling depending upon colour would have to be replaced

by others. Characters depending upon colour, whereby at present we readily distinguish one thing from another—suppose a wholesome from a poisonous plant —would have to give place to some other, perhaps much less convenient, means of discrimination. Still, as I said, we might, on the whole, get on very fairly. Indeed, while an abnormal deviation from the normal sensation of colour is by no means rare, there are a few cases on record, though it is true very few, in which the person appeared to see only one colour, whatever the sensation of that one colour may have been to him, and yet such persons have gone about among their fellow-men without any very serious inconvenience.

Accordingly, when we regard the sensation of colour, and all that follows from our possession of such a sensation, we are led to connect it rather with the enjoyments than with the necessities of life. In studying the construction of the eye in relation to the perception of form, we found indications of such elaborate and minute contrivances for connecting the external object with the sensorium that, utterly unable as we are to connect any influence on the bodily structure with the mental sensation, the evidence of design seems overwhelming; or at least I may say that such I think it would to the minds of most persons who were able to follow the evidence. We have not the same evidence, so far as it depends on structure, with regard to the perception of colour, for, in fact, we know next to nothing about it. The simplest theory which falls in with what we know of the laws of the perception of colour is, I think, that of Dr. Young, according to which we have three primary sensations of colour, and these are in general excited simultaneously by light of any kind presented to us, but in relative proportions differing according to the refrangibility of the light so presented in case it be homogeneous, or the refrangibilities of its constituents· in case it be mixed. Young's theory has received a remarkable confirmation from the researches of Maxwell, who, by careful quantitative experiments, carried out partly by his own eyes, partly by those of various other individuals, showed that any colour might be expressed by means of three colours taken as standards, in such a sense that a match might always be established, and *that* in one definite way, according that is to definite proportions, between one of the four colours against the other three, or else two against the remaining two. This no doubt might be equally true whether the triplicity were objective, residing in the quality of the light itself, or subjective, indicating a triplicity in our own sensations. But as there is no phenomenon indicating any such triplicity in light itself, and the theory of undulations, now so well established, does not leave room for any such, we are led to refer the triplicity

which had long been noticed to a triplicity of our
own sensations, as Young was the first to do; and
an objective triplicity being excluded, the quantitative
experiments of Maxwell confirmed, as I said, the
subjective theory of Young, showing as they did that
lights which matched in colour and intensity, though
they were by no means physically identical, were
nevertheless interchangeable in the sense that, on
adding them to the same third light, a light giving
the same sensation was produced in either case.
But what the mechanism for the excitement of the
three primary sensations may be, we do not at present
know, and therefore if we regard, as I think we
should be led to regard, the production of these
three primary sensations as designed, the evidence of
design arises from a consideration of the objects
accomplished, strengthened by our observation of
the contrivances which, in various other analogous
cases, we are to a greater or less extent able to
follow.

Admitting then that the reference of beneficial
objects accomplished is not to be ruled out of court,
I think we shall be led to regard the beauty of the
colours and coloured markings of flowers and birds
and butterflies, etc., as designed to be a source of
pleasure to the beholders. There may be other ends
accomplished more directly connected with the wellbeing of the living thing on which the beautiful

markings are found—such, for example, as the fertilisation of flowers, by attracting bees and other insects
which carry the pollen from flower to flower.
But after making all due allowance for such con-
current advantages, I cannot help thinking that a
large residue must be left which we are obliged to
regard as arranged for the purpose of affording
pleasure by the beauty of the object. Nor need we
confine our ideas of the appreciation of beauty to
man, though of course, when we pass to the minds
of the lower animals, much must be matter of conjecture. Still, there is nothing unreasonable in
supposing that they too are able in a way to take
pleasure in the exercise of their sense of sight on
the objects which to us appear so beautiful, though
it may be without self-consciousness, or knowledge
of what it is that gives them pleasure. But even
if we decline to indulge in such conjectures, and
confine ourselves to the mind of man, of which we
do know something by experience, it will suffice for
my purpose. We see on all sides provision for the
material wellbeing of living things, be they animals
or plants; some of them so important for their
welfare that without them even the life of the individual could scarcely be maintained, let alone the
species to which the individual belongs continued in
apparently indefinite succession. That there should
be provision, not merely for the sustentation and

generally for the material wellbeing of the creature, but also for its enjoyment and the brightness of its life, exalts, as it seems to me, our ideas of the benevolence of the Creator.

Of course there are plenty of objects of beauty in things which neither are nor ever were possessed of life; take, for example, the colours of the rainbow, the clouds near sunset, and so forth. But these we recognise as the inevitable result of certain simple laws which we can investigate, and even in many cases subject to mathematical calculation, and the evidence of design does not, I think, strike one in the same way as when we are dealing with the beautiful markings of a flower, or of the wing of a butterfly, which, so far as we know or can conceive, might just as well have been absent.

But it may be said, Does not this prove the fallacy of the whole argument? Have we any right to establish a distinction between beautiful phenomena brought about by the inevitable operation of the fundamental laws of optics, and those of which we can give no such explanation, nor even see any indication of a probable explanation?

I think the answer to this question must be, For aught we know to the contrary, if we were acquainted with all the principles involved, the distinction we have drawn might disappear. But does it follow from this that the argument for design which, in the

one case, appeared to have much force, must be
given up, because in the other case it appeared to
strike us less forcibly? I think not. I will endeavour to illustrate the view I should be disposed to
take of it by reference to something in ordinary life
that we can well understand.

Suppose a person who was a perfect master in
some far-reaching and abstruse branch of science.
Suppose there was another person to whom it was
of great importance that he should be acquainted
with a few of the leading principles of the science,
with a view, we will suppose, to some practical purpose, but who had neither the leisure nor the ability
to go into the science beyond taking in a few of the
leading principles. His instructor would defeat his
own object if he were to crowd the pupil's head with
all the details of the science, with all the exceptions
to the *direct* application of general principles, arising
out of peculiar conditions of a recondite nature,
which, at first sight, might look like exceptions to
the general principles themselves. In many cases
he would purposely keep out of view qualifications
to a general statement which he was perfectly aware
were requisite in special instances. And the connection of different branches of the subject with one
another, and of the subject, as a whole, with other
branches of science, which he himself perfectly understood, might be a thing altogether above the com-

prehension of the pupil. And yet the information which the pupil received from his teacher might be the very thing he wanted—might fit him for his post in a manner that could not have been brought about if the teacher had bewildered him with details or generalities, of which he could form but the haziest notion. Yet the pupil's knowledge might be perfectly sound as far as it went—might suffice for the various applications of fundamental principles which it concerned him to make.

Now it seems to me that the evidence of design arising out of the beauty of forms and markings, for the existence of which we can give no account as a necessary result of laws with which we are acquainted, and which, in many cases, appear to fulfil no object beyond the gratification which the sight of them affords, stands upon much the same sort of footing as the pupil's acceptance of the general principles that he had been taught, in the illustration which I have ventured to give. The pupil, we may imagine, is fairly sensible of the limitation of his knowledge. Perhaps, in some limited branch of the subject, his knowledge may extend a good deal further; he may perceive that other conditions require to be taken into account, modifying the results which, at first sight, would seem to follow from general principles. He might suppose, naturally enough, that if he were more thoroughly acquainted with the other branches of his subject, the necessity would be seen of modifying, in certain cases, the conclusions which, at first sight, he might have been disposed to draw from the general principles which he had been taught. But surely he would be entirely wrong if, in consequence of the occasional modifications which were found necessary in the one branch which he did know pretty well, he were to reject as worthless the general principles which he had been taught in all the other branches.

In a similar manner, it seems to me, we are not warranted in rejecting the evidence of design in beauty afforded by the markings and colours of flowers, feathers, etc., merely because we may conjecture (it cannot be more than conjecture) that if we knew everything about the laws of growth and nutrition of living things, those markings, etc., would be seen to be as much an inevitable consequence of the supposed laws as the colours of the rainbow are of the laws of the refraction and dispersion of light, combined with capillary attraction, which keeps the falling drops in a spherical form.

I do not, observe, say that even if we had that ideal knowledge that has just been supposed, the argument for design would have to be abandoned. It would however, I think, assume a somewhat different character, on which I do not at present pro-

pose to dwell. But we need not spend time in first
placing ourselves in imagination in a purely ideal
condition, in which neither we nor our successors,
so far as we can judge, are in the least likely to find
themselves, and then inquiring how we should act
under these purely imaginary circumstances. We
have quite enough to exercise our minds in the
world in which we actually live without transporting ourselves to fairy land. Indeed, it would not
have been worth while to mention at all the subject
on which I have briefly touched, were it not to anticipate a possible objection—an objection which is
not so very unlikely to be raised, since the rapid
progress of science has some tendency to create a feeling as if the whole system of nature were explicable
(though, of course, nobody could say explained) by
purely scientific methods.

Assuming, then, the validity of the evidence of
design afforded by beauty as such, and not merely
in relation to some collateral advantage secured
thereby—such, for example, as the fertilisation of
flowers by means of insects that are attracted by
their bright colours—we gain, I think, an enhanced
idea of the Divine benevolence. We see provision,
not merely for the continued existence and healthy
activity of the creature, but even for what we may
call its mental enjoyment. I use the expression
"what we may call," because we commonly speak

of mental enjoyment with reference to the human race; whereas it seems likely, though, of course, we cannot prove it, that even lower races are not incapable of receiving satisfaction from the sight of objects of beauty.

LECTURE V

Contrast between the structure of living things and general physical laws in relation to the argument for design—Chemical substances—Laws of chemical combination—Atomic theory—Question of the possible formation of the elements by chemical combination from one primordial kind of matter—Even such an evolutionary origin of the elements still postulates the existence and similarity of the atoms of the primordial matter.

IN my last Lecture I raised the question whether the beneficial results, which we can deduce as necessary consequences of a few fundamental laws, can be appealed to as affording evidence of design in the same manner as the exquisitely elaborate construction of some organ, such, for example, as our organ of sight, for the existence of which, as a necessary consequence of known causes, we are utterly unable to give any account, but which, at the same time, fulfils its functions in a manner that fills us more and more with admiration the more we examine into it.

Questions of this kind, which border on metaphysics, are of such a kind that probably persons whose minds are of different complexions would be disposed to give to them answers differing more or

less. I cannot pretend to be any authority in matters
of this nature, and I could only say how the thing
appears to my own mind. To me it seems that the
evidence is more direct and palpable in the latter
case than in the former; and that it is after we have
dwelt on these more direct and palpable instances
that we are best prepared to enter on the consideration of instances of the former class. Moreover, the
contemplations to which we are led are not quite the
same in the two cases. In the first case, as we know
nothing of any method by which the result might be
brought about—that is, know nothing of any forces
competent to build up and direct the building up
of the structure—the mind is not diverted from the
conception of design, and consequently of mind, not
only devising but able to execute the foreordained
plan; in the latter, we are rather led to contemplate
the system which we find in nature as a whole; to
admire the way in which the whole, as a whole, is
conducive to the welfare of man, and generally of all
living things; while, at the same time, the operation
of those general laws according to which that whole
is constructed is not necessarily of direct utility in
each particular, considered as isolated from the system of which it forms a part.

Having made these preliminary remarks, I proceed now to consider in more detail some one branch

of physical science. I have already briefly touched
on the subject of the luminiferous ether, though it
is true, not so much with regard to the important
offices which it fulfils, as on account of its all-
pervading presence and of its mysterious nature, and
of the hints bearing on natural theology, which may
be derived therefrom. I have alluded, though still
more briefly, to universal gravitation. In this last
subject, beginning it may be with an object close at
hand, and of moderate size—such as an apple falling
from a tree, which, it is said, first suggested the
theory to the mind of Newton—we are led step by
step up to the contemplation and even measurement
of masses of matter—such as those of the earth and
planets, and of the sun itself—so vast that the arith-
metical values which express them do not at first
enable us to appreciate their immensity. I propose
to-day to touch on another branch of science, in
which, beginning as before with masses of matter
close at hand, and of moderate size, we are led on to
the contemplation of magnitudes almost inconceivably small.

It seems almost necessary that I should say a
few words by way of introduction on a subject
which is now so trite that I am a little afraid of
wearying you; I allude to the nature of a chemical
substance and of chemical composition and decomposition.

To be entitled to the designation of a chemical substance, a substance must, in the first place, be uniform throughout, though not necessarily throughout in the same state of aggregation. Thus a mass of pure water is the same in one part of the mass as in another, and the same from whatever source the water be derived. But if a closed space—say a sealed glass globe—be partly filled with water, and contain nothing else—that is, no other kind of ponderable matter—we may, by the application of cold, convert a portion· of the water into ice, and then the whole will no longer be homogeneous, and the ice and the water may easily be mechanically separated. But we have not by these means divided the mass into two portions of matter of different properties; for if we apply heat to the ice we convert it into water, of absolutely the same properties as that which remained unfrozen, and if we apply cold to the latter we convert it into ice of just the same properties as that which was obtained in the first instance. Similar remarks apply to the conversion of water into the state of an elastic fluid (steam), and the re-conversion of that into water.

But the fact of a mass of water being homogeneous throughout does not constitute it a chemical substance. Thus alcohol and water may be poured into the same vessel and thoroughly mixed, and the liquid thus obtained is the same in all respects in

one part of it as in another.   Yet it is not a chemical
substance.   For, in the first place, two such mixtures
made independently are not in general identical with
each other in their properties; they are not so unless
the proportions of water and alcohol used are the
same in the two cases.   By gradually changing those
proportions in successive operations, we should obtain
a series of liquids of properties gradually changing
from those of alcohol to those of water.   And, in the
second place, by distilling the liquid and collecting
separately successive portions as they come over, we
obtain a series of liquids permanently differing from
one another, the first portions nearly resembling
alcohol and the last portions water.   And if we
knew nothing of the history of the liquid first
presented to us (which we have hitherto been supposing was formed by mixing alcohol and water), still
by subjecting it to distillation, as above described,
we should be led to the conclusion that it was not a
chemical substance but a mixture.

By various methods, more or less analogous to
those which I have just mentioned, it is concluded,
sometimes, indeed, only as a probability, but generally
as practically a certainty, that such or such a substance is what is called a chemical substance, or that
it is only a mixture, as the case may be.   The
substance under examination may be a solid, or a
liquid, or a gas, or it may be known under two,

or under all three, of these conditions. The air
we breathe, making abstraction of certain impurities
or admixtures of very small amount, and also of the
small but variable quantity of water which it contains, is found to be everywhere the same in all
its properties, or at any rate extremely nearly so ;
but it is not, for all that, a chemical substance, but a
mixture, formed of two gases—oxygen and nitrogen—
merely blended together. The water we drink, on
the other hand, making as before abstraction of
minute impurities, is not only the same in its nature
under all circumstances, but is incapable of being
resolved into two or more different substances, which
by their mere mixture produce it.

But now we come to the consideration of a
process in some respects agreeing with the mixture
of two substances forming a third, the mixture
itself, but in other respects utterly and completely
different. I allude to chemical change, to chemical
composition or decomposition, as the case may be.

To take an instance of this, let us recur to water.
I have said that air is mainly a mixture of the two
gases—oxygen and nitrogen—each of which is a single
chemical substance. There is another gas, also a
single, unmixed substance, called hydrogen, the
lightest of all known gases. The two gases—oxygen
and hydrogen—may be mixed in all proportions just
like alcohol and water; and, just as in the case of

the liquid formed by mixing these two latter liquids, the mixture of those two gases is a gas, the specific gravity and other properties of which gradually and insensibly change from those of pure oxygen to those of pure hydrogen, as the proportion of hydrogen, at first infinitesimal, is gradually increased, till at last it is the proportion of oxygen that becomes infinitesimal.

But now suppose that when the proportions are such that neither gas greatly predominates over the other, a light is applied to a minute portion of the mixture, immediately a flame passes almost instantaneously over the whole mixture, accompanied by a sudden but almost momentary expansion, causing a violent explosion, and as a result of this change we have exactly the same weight of matter left in our hands as before, but that matter is totally different from what we had before. It consists of an elastic fluid, which quickly condenses into a well-known liquid, no other than water, while a portion of one or other of the original gases is left outstanding, unless the original gases happened to have been mixed in a definite proportion, always the same, in which case no substance but water is found as the outcome of the change which had taken place.

It is remarkable that the quantities of the two gases which must be mixed together, in order that nothing but water may be the product, are connected by a very simple relation. The volume of the hydrogen must be just double that of the oxygen; and if the quantity of hydrogen in the mixture exceed this, the excess of its volume over the double of the volume of oxygen is found as hydrogen after the explosion has taken place; while if the quantity of hydrogen originally taken was less in volume than double the volume of the oxygen, then the overplus of gas after the explosion is found to be oxygen instead of hydrogen, and its volume is found to be the excess of its original volume over half the volume of the hydrogen taken.

Here, then, we have the remarkable result that a substance is produced utterly different in its properties from those of the substances originally taken, or from any mere mixture of the two. Moreover, the change from the one condition to the other is accompanied by very remarkable phenomena: by the production of light and heat, by a great exhibition of mechanical power.

The same combination is effected, continuously instead of explosively, if a mixture of the two gases is burnt in a suitable jet, and the heat thus produced is one of the most powerful sources of heat known, readily fusing highly refractory substances, such, for instance, as platinum.

As the union of the two gases forms water, so conversely water may be decomposed into the two. The

most direct way of effecting this, though not the first
to be discovered, consists in the simple application of
heat. Thus, when fused platinum is poured into water
a large quantity of gas is evolved, which consists of a
mixture of oxygen and hydrogen just in the proportion
to form water.

We have here an instance of both processes—the
chemical combination of two different bodies to form
a third of quite different properties from those of
either of the original bodies, and again the decomposition of a single chemical substance into two
others, of which it is, as it is said, composed. And
it is to be noticed that the combination is accompanied by a development of energy, by the setting
free of the energy which may be looked on as having
lain hid in the mixed gases prior to combination.
And we know that the converse process—that of
the decomposition of water into the two gases of
which it is formed—cannot take place without a
consumption of energy, though in the particular
form in which the decomposition has been mentioned
as taking place this consumption of energy, derived
from the heat of the fused platinum, could not easily
be experimentally demonstrated.

I may mention here, that in chemical combinations in general, as in the above particular instance,
energy previously latent in the substances which
are about to combine is set free, so as to be exhibited

by development of heat, mechanical force, etc. I
have said " in general," because the usual rule is not
without exceptions, apparent at least. There are
some cases in which energy is set free when a
compound substance is resolved into the substances
of which it is composed. Yet even here the exception may be more apparent than real. For it seems
probable that the separation of the substances from
each other may be accompanied by an act of self-
combination of the substances so separated; but this
is a matter of which I cannot at present do more
than give a hint.

Though I have described chemical combination in
only one particular instance—that of oxygen and
hydrogen to form water—it is a process which is
constantly going on in nature, as well as constantly
employed in the arts and manufactures. It is constantly going on in our own bodies, and is essential
to the continuance of our lives.

To go back to the case of water. We have seen
that it is capable of being resolved into two gases,
and the question naturally arises—Are these gases
themselves, or is either of them, capable of being
resolved into two or more substances, of which it
is a chemical compound? As to the answer to
this question, all we can say is, that up to the
present time they have each resisted all attempts
so to resolve them, and we have not any evidence

that they are capable of being so resolved. These substances are accordingly regarded as elements.

The same designation is applied to the various chemical substances which have resisted all attempts to decompose them. We do not, of course, assume that they never can be decomposed; still less that we never shall obtain evidence of their composite nature, even though we might not be able actually to decompose them. It is remarkable that as our knowledge progresses, so far from the number of elements being reduced by showing that some are only stable compounds of certain of the others, it is actually considerably increased, by the discovery from time to time of fresh elements. At present there are as many as about seventy known, those recently discovered being rare substances found in small quantities, even if, as sometimes happens, widely distributed in almost infinitesimally small proportions. Yet in the present state of our knowledge each comes before us in a manner analogous to an arbitrary constant in mathematics.

I shall have occasion to return to this subject later on; but for the present I will confine myself to a few of the commonest and most widely distributed of the elements.

I have said that air was in the main a mixture of the two gases, oxygen and nitrogen. But just as oxygen and hydrogen are capable of chemically combining, forming thereby a substance (water) altogether different in its properties from either of its elements, so oxygen and nitrogen are capable of combining, and that in different proportions, forming a series of different chemical substances, differing in their properties from the original elements and from each other. Unlike, however, oxygen and hydrogen, the pair of gases we are now considering do not spontaneously combine, not even in presence of a light, and their direct combination is only with difficulty effected; and it is by indirect processes that their compounds are obtained. As many as five such compounds are known, though some of these, it is true, not by themselves, but only in further combination with something else, be it only water. Now a remarkably simple law regulates the proportions in which the two gases combine. The weights of oxygen which combine with the same weight of nitrogen to form the different compounds are in the proportion of the numbers, 1, 2, 3, 4, 5. A similar law is found to hold good generally in the combination of any two elements which do combine, so that if we take the weights of the two which combine to form one of the compounds, the proportion of the weights in any other compound is that of a simple multiple of the weight of the first element to another simple multiple of the weight of the second element. It would lead me much too far from my subject to enter into any detail, or to discuss the question of the best choice to make of a compound of two elements to start with, so as to express in the simplest manner the compositions of the other compounds, or to point out how, in certain cases, such compounds are rather to be regarded as compounds of compounds. It will be sufficient for my purpose to take the three elements already mentioned—namely, oxygen, hydrogen, and nitrogen. Hydrogen, I may mention, like nitrogen is able to combine with oxygen in more than one proportion; a second compound is known, and just as in the case of nitrogen a simple law connects the proportions of oxygen in the two compounds with hydrogen: the proportion of oxygen which unites with hydrogen in that second compound is just double of what it is in water.

Till lately, only one compound of nitrogen and hydrogen was known, ammonia. Now, if we take the commonest compound of oxygen and hydrogen— namely, water—and one of the compounds of oxygen and nitrogen—say laughing gas—it is found that the proportion of the weight of oxygen to that of the other gas in the compound is 8 to 1 in the first case, and 4 to 7 in the second. We see, then, that the same weight 8 of the element which is common to both—namely, oxygen—combines with a weight 1 of hydrogen and a weight 14 of nitrogen. Now if we inquire what are the proportions by weight of nitrogen and hydrogen in the compound ammonia, we find that they are as 14 to 3. That is to say, the combining weight of hydrogen with a given weight of nitrogen, to form ammonia, may be inferred from its combining weight with oxygen, and of that again with nitrogen, except as to the multiplier 3, a low integer.

I have endeavoured briefly, and I fear imperfectly, to put before you the experimental facts on which Dalton's atomic theory, now universally accepted, ultimately rests. They are, first, the law of definite proportions; secondly, the law of multiple proportions; thirdly, the law of chemical equivalents. All these laws are comprehended in the theory.

We cannot geometrically conceive of space otherwise than as infinitely divisible. However small a volume we take, we cannot help conceiving of it as divisible into two, and either portion, when so divided, as being itself divisible into two, and so on indefinitely. I said, "However small a volume we take;" but, in truth, there is no such thing as greatness or smallness absolutely considered. When we speak of a volume, or an area, or a length, as being great or small, it is always by comparison with something else.

Now, instead of considering mere space, let us contemplate a limited portion of space filled with matter of some one kind, and let it be of a kind which we cannot, by any means at our disposal, divide into two; let it, for example, be hydrogen. Suppose we have a closed vessel filled with this gas. We may divide it into two by a partition, and that again into two, and so on, and yet, as far as we can actually carry the experiment, the gas in each portion will have the same properties as before. As far as we can carry on the actual experiment, there appears to be no more limit to the divisibility of hydrogen than there is to that of space in our geometrical conceptions. But in order to account for the laws of chemical combination, Dalton supposed that there is in the nature of things really a limit to this subdivision; that the gas consists of ultimate portions which can no longer be divided, or at least not without ceasing to be the same chemical substance as before; that these ultimate portions, or *molecules,* as they are now called, are all alike, but so minute, that any portion of the gas which we can actually examine contains a number of them so vast as to be for all ordinary purposes practically infinite. The same constitution would, of course, apply to the other chemical elements, so that oxygen, for example, would be an assemblage of a vast number of molecules, like one another, but differing altogether from those of hydrogen, and so on in other cases.

The same molecular constitution of matter which we have supposed to exist in the elements—that is,

in chemical substances which we are unable to resolve—would naturally extend to those which we can
form or resolve. Thus, for instance, water, though
apparently infinitely divisible like space, must be supposed in like manner to be made up of ultimate molecules which cannot be further divided without ceasing
to be water—without, that is, being such that an
aggregate of a vast number of them would no longer be
water, but something quite different in its properties.

Since, then, water consists of molecules all alike,
and is formed in some way by the union of oxygen
and hydrogen, it follows that its molecule must be
composed in some simple way of those of oxygen
and hydrogen. Whatever this way may be, as it
must be always the same, it follows that the proportion by weight in which the two bodies combine to
form water will be invariable, which accords with
the law of definite proportion.   That law alone gives
us no information as to how the molecule of water
is built up.   Perhaps we might have thought it most
likely, as being apparently the most simple, to suppose that single molecules of the two gases combined
to form a single molecule of the compound.   There
are, however, reasons, into which I cannot enter, for
believing that when chemical substances are in the
state of gas or vapour, equal volumes of the different
substances under standard conditions of pressure and
temperature contain equal numbers of molecules.

We infer from this that two molecules of hydrogen
combine with one of oxygen to form water. But as
the volume of the water formed, when in the state
of vapour under standard conditions, is the same as
that of the hydrogen employed, twice therefore that
of the oxygen, it is inferred that the molecule of
oxygen is made up of two perfectly similar halves,
which, though they cannot be separated so as to
be exhibited apart by themselves, are nevertheless
separated when the gas combines with hydrogen.
We may picture to ourselves a pair of molecules of
hydrogen as pulling asunder a molecule of oxygen,
and appropriating the two halves to themselves. As
no further subdivision of the molecule of oxygen is
indicated by the quantity of oxygen which is contained in any gaseous compound into which that
element enters, the half molecule of oxygen is regarded as an atom. Similar considerations apply to
a variety of other elements. We see at once how
the atomic theory accounts for the law of definite
proportions, as regards which chemical combination
so notably differs from mere mixture.

The theory lends itself with equal readiness to an
explanation of the law of multiple proportions. Not
to go beyond the combination of the same two gases,
there is a second compound known—the peroxide of
hydrogen—in which the proportion by weight of the
oxygen, which combines with a given weight of

hydrogen, is just double what it is in water. This
is in perfect accordance with what we should expect
from the atomic theory. In fact, the simplest conception that we could form of a compound of the
two bodies, looking *merely* to the atomic theory, is
to suppose that a single molecule of one of the elements combined with a single molecule of the other,
to form a single molecule of the compound. This would
give the combining proportion actually observed,
though it does not follow that such is the exact
constitution of the compound. One of its molecules
might, for example, be formed of two half molecules,
or atoms, of the two gases; or, again, of a pair of
molecules of the one united with a pair of molecules of the other. The three suppositions I have
just made seem to lie in decreasing order of probability; but in default of a direct determination of
the vapour density of the compound, which, so far
as I know, has not yet been made, we should hardly
be justified in pronouncing in favour of one of the
suppositions to the exclusion of the others.

Lastly, the theory accounts in the simplest manner
for the law of chemical equivalents. Thus, since
oxygen and hydrogen combine in the proportion of
8 to 1 to form water, and oxygen and nitrogen combine in the proportion of 8 to 14 to form laughing
gas, it follows that the ratio of the weights of the
molecules of hydrogen and nitrogen must be either

1 to 14, or simply related thereto; and accordingly, if hydrogen and nitrogen combine, it must be in the proportion of 1 to 14, or of a low multiple of one of those numbers to a low multiple of the other. In the long-known compound ammonia it is actually 3 to 14.

The very same laws of combination of two ele-ments with each other to form a compound, apply also to the combination of compounds with one another to form compounds of greater complexity.

The question now naturally arises—What are we to think of the so-called elements? We are utterly unable to decompose them. If we assume the crea-tion of matter, must we therefore suppose each ele-ment to have been a separate creation? Or, on the other hand, may we suppose that combination and decomposition is capable in the nature of things of being carried backwards as well as forwards, and that the so-called elements may have thus been formed by some evolutionary process from a much simpler condi-tion of things, perhaps by a process of self-combination in different ways from one primordial element?

Our inability to decompose the substances which we call elements does not seem to afford any very strong argument against the latter supposition. Thus chemists recognised from analogy the existence of the element fluorine before it had been even partially separated, and even now the properties of the ele-ment in the separate state are but imperfectly known.

The difficulty in this case is, however, not so much to separate it, as to find a suitable vessel which will hold it without being attacked by it. But there is another, and probably still more formidable, difficulty standing in the way of any great extension of further decomposition.

As a rule, the most intense exhibitions of the energy of combination are manifested in the combination of elementary bodies, or of bodies composed in a simple manner of the elements. Hence, if the so-called elements are in reality compounds of bodies still more elementary, we should expect the combining energy of those still simpler bodies to be extremely intense, and their compounds, the so-called elements, to be so very stable, that it is doubtful whether any means that the chemist possesses, or that he could even possibly devise, would suffice for their separation. And if we could imagine them separated, it is doubtful whether any material could be found which would be available for making a vessel which could contain them, as not being itself attacked. On both accounts it seems very doubtful whether much, if any, progress is likely to be made in the way of decomposing the substances which we provisionally at least regard as elements.

But though the actual decomposition of the elements seems to be of very doubtful prospect, it is quite conceivable that some theory of the constitution of the elements may be discovered which is supported by such a weight of evidence as to ensure general assent.

No such theory is at present known, but there appear to be some indications pointing more or less doubtfully in that direction. I will mention one. The relative molecular weights of the various elements form a series of constants of fundamental importance in chemistry, and their determination with as much accuracy as possible, by methods gradually improved, has naturally engaged the attention of many distinguished chemists. It was suggested by Dr. Prout that the molecular weights of the various elements were multiples of the smallest of them— namely, that of hydrogen. Comparatively recent determinations of the relative molecular weights of some of the most important elements have led to numbers so remarkably close to multiples of that of hydrogen, that attention has been revived to Prout's hypothesis; while, in other cases, it would seem that the supposition in its original form can hardly be maintained, though possibly it may be if we so modify it as to admit multiples of half, or, as may perhaps be necessary, a quarter of the molecular weight of hydrogen.

If we suppose chemical combination to extend backwards from the so-called elements, so as to derive them from a smaller number of bodies still more elementary, and so on, till at last we arrive at a single form of matter, it is obvious that the molecular weights of all the substances which are regarded as elements must be commensurable; in other words, that they all admit of a common divisor. Whether they do, without having recourse to so small a divisor that the unavoidable errors of experiment prevent us from saying whether the weights to be examined are, or are not, multiples of that divisor, must for the present be left an open question.

It might, perhaps, be regarded at first sight as a strong objection to the supposition of the derivation of the so-called elements, by a backward extension of the laws of chemical composition, from a single primordial form of matter, that the most energetic chemical combinations that we actually witness take place between very dissimilar substances, and therefore we should not expect very stable compounds to be formed out of one and the same material. But to this objection there is an obvious answer. How is it that the very great energy of combination, for instance, of oxygen and hydrogen is manifested? Why, the gases are prepared separately, then mixed together, and on combination being started by a spark an explosion occurs. We know that at a sufficiently high temperature water is resolved into its elements. Suppose that we started with the gases mixed together at a temperature above that

in question, and that the temperature of the vessel
containing them was then gradually lowered till it
was reduced to the temperature of the air.   On
arriving at the temperature of dissociation, the gases
would quietly combine, forming steam, which, as the
temperature was still further reduced, would pass
by successive portions into water.   There would be
nothing in the *direct* phenomena to indicate the
great energy of the combination.   The reason why
it is so strikingly manifested in the ordinary experiment is that the two gases are kept apart, and then
brought together under conditions in which the
great energy of combination is capable of manifestation.   But while different kinds of matter may
be kept apart, matter of a given kind must always
be in presence of itself, and therefore there is not
the opportunity for the direct manifestation of great
energy of combination if it exists.   Suppose, for
example, that at a suitable temperature atomic
oxygen could exist as a permanent gas, a gas the
molecule of which would be half that of oxygen,
and which, therefore, according to known laws,
would have a density half that of oxygen.   Then it
is quite conceivable, I should think highly probable,
that if combination were started, in some such way,
suppose, as in a mixture of hydrogen and oxygen,
there would be a manifestation of intense energy
of combination.   But whether the substance could

possibly exist without self - combination, unless, perhaps, at some enormously high temperature, is very doubtful.

These considerations, it seems to me, prevent us from ruling out of court the supposition that all chemical substances are formed, in accordance with the laws of chemical combination, from some one primordial form of matter.

The two extreme suppositions between which we are shut in as to the chemical constitution of matter are: (1) That the elements of the chemist are radically distinct kinds of matter, which cannot, even theoretically, be formed by chemical combination from forms of matter yet more elementary still; (2) that they are all formed by chemical combination from one primordial kind of matter.

On the first supposition, the elements of the chemist, notwithstanding the largeness of their number, come before us, to use an illustration I have already employed, like so many arbitrary and independent constants in mathematics. On this supposition we cannot help wondering why some of them, especially some of the rare earths which have of late years been engaging the attention of chemists, should ever have existed at all. From their rarity they can apparently have little influence on the system of nature as a whole, nor do they appear, so far as we know, to be of any use beyond exercising chemists in the study of their subject. On the second supposition, we may look on their formation as a sort of by-play, arising, accidentally as it were, in an evolutionary process whereby the elements of the chemist were built up from the atoms of the supposed primordial matter.

But whether we adopt the first or the second of the above suppositions, or something intermediate between them, we arrive at last at a stage beyond which our chemical laws, even though we extend them beyond the point which we can reach by actual experiment, fail us, and we are brought face to face with ultimate atoms, be they all of one kind, or be they of a limited number of different kinds. What those ultimate atoms are, we know not, and why they should all be alike to one another, or, at least, all of each kind, if there be different kinds, we know not. To use an expression of Sir John Herschel's, quoted by Maxwell, they have all the appearance of manufactured articles. The speculations of Lord Kelvin as to their being vortex atoms do not help us at all in accounting for their identity with one another, as he, I doubt not, would be the first to allow.

What the nature of the forces may be whereby atoms and molecules combine together to form more complex molecules, and in doing so give out energy, we do not know. But we know very well that

chemical combination plays a most important part
in our welfare, nay, in the very continuance of our
lives from minute to minute. The inanimate world
presents us chiefly with the results of its action
in past ages. Or, at least, we have a vast variety
of substances ready to our hands which we *might*,
of course, imagine to have been created as we find
them. But in face of the evidence of past changes
which the earth underwent by the operation in
past ages of causes still at work, though probably
having a far greater scope for action in a much
earlier condition of the earth, and in the face of
the evidence which astronomy affords of changes
even now going on in some of the heavenly bodies—
changes pointing to a still earlier condition than
what geology can deal with,—in the face, I say, of
these things, it seems more reasonable to suppose
that the earth, in the condition in which it now
is, was evolved under the action of chemical and
mechanical forces from a much simpler condition;
possibly even from a condition in which primordial
matter had not yet entered into chemical combination. As a result of this past action, we find
solids containing the mineral matters required for
the growth of plants, rocks even now disintegrating,
and so keeping up the fertility of soils, metallic ores
collected into particular places, so as to be available
for the wants of man.

But it is with reference to life that chemical combination and decomposition are of such essential and continuous importance. We know how quickly our lives come to an end if we are deprived of air, even though it be by the substitution for air of a gas, such as nitrogen, which is not poisonous in itself. In such a case death ensues simply in consequence of the exclusion of oxygen, which, in the normal condition, enters into a sort of loose chemical combination with the colouring matter of the blood, which itself had been previously deprived of a portion of its oxygen, reduced, as it is called, by communication of the oxygen it had received in a previous passage through the lungs to substances present in the blood, which were derived from the food taken in and digested. This oxidation, forming a sort of slow combustion going on in the circulating blood, keeps up the supply of animal heat; while, at the same time, a transformation of the food, which takes place under the chemical changes belonging to digestion, continually replenishes the blood, and enables the cycle of changes that has been referred to to be kept up.

The food of animals is derived, directly or indirectly, from vegetables. But whereas the changes in the animal body that we have been considering involve an expenditure of energy, the series of changes that we have had in contemplation

could not be kept up if it were the same with
vegetables—that is to say, if the various changes
which they undergo involved, like those in the
animal body, a continual consumption of energy.
Here, then, an additional factor comes in; there
is a continual supply of energy to the plant, which
is derived from the sun's radiation. Under the
influence of light a series of chemical changes take
place in the growing plant, which are of such a
kind as could not take place spontaneously, that is,
without a supply from the outside, inasmuch as
they demand a constant supply of energy from
without.

The upshot is, that while chemical combination is
of essential importance, it is yet but a portion of a
vast system of transformations the several parts of
which dovetail into one another in a marvellous
manner, and in the end are conducive to the maintenance of the life and to the welfare of man and of
the animal kingdom generally.

The same might be said of pretty nearly every
branch of physical science. But, as I remarked at
the outset, for the object of these Lectures there is
no need to multiply examples, the same inferences
in a general way are deducible from one branch of
physical science as from another. I reserve to my
next Lecture some applications of the physical considerations which have occupied our attention to-day.

LECTURE VI

IN my previous Lectures I brought before you two instances, in one of which results of the utmost importance to man, and not to man alone, were brought about by a highly elaborate structure, of the formation of which we were unable to give any account, I mean to exhibit it as an outcome of natural causes, while in the other results, at least as important, were brought about through a chain of natural causation, or, at least, in great measure through such a chain, the following out of which carried us far back to a condition of things as remote as possible from the final beneficial effects.

In the case of the human eye—and something similar applies to the eyes of other animals—besides the optical structure, resembling the telescope of an optician, by which images were formed on the retina, we had in the retina itself an arrangement of the most exquisite character for receiving separate impressions of the various points of the object, even when they were so near one another as to be separated by an angular interval of only one minute or so, and for connecting these impressions, by means of nerve fibres, in a manner which we can only imperfectly follow, with the brain, which we have reason to suppose is the seat of the sensation. Not only so, but we had an elaborate contrivance for adjusting the motions of the eyeballs in their sockets so as to secure singleness of vision with the two eyes, notwithstanding a very frequent transference of aim, in the field of view, demanding a rotation of the eyeballs in their sockets. And yet we know of no second causes, as we call them, capable of bringing about such structures as these. In saying this, of course, I am aware that there are some who think they are explicable by the theory of natural selection— explicable, that is, in the sense of being referable to known laws of which they are the outcome.

With reference to this attempt at an explanation, I can only say that it is very far indeed from being satisfactory to my own mind. I do not intend to argue the question, more especially as in things of this nature, in regard to the appearance of force in the argument, very much depends on the idiosyncrasy of each particular mind. To me, I confess, the attempt to explain the result in this way seems like a desperate effort to refer it at all costs to second causes. I do not for a moment affirm that there are not second causes at work; it seems to me likely enough that there are. But I prefer to confess my ignorance of such till I meet, if ever I do, something more satisfactory. If there be any truth in the view which I ventured to broach in a former Lecture, that there is about living things something of the nature of a directing power, under the influence of which their structures are built up, it would seem more natural to look in that direction for an explanation. Whether we shall ever get to know anything of the laws of action of that power, if such a power exists, seems to be very doubtful indeed. But if it does exist, and we ignore its existence, we shall only be led away from a true explanation of the phenomena which present themselves.

The other instance to which I referred just now is that of the results brought about by chemical action. It is true that of the origin of chemical action itself we know nothing; but as regards the molecular constitution of matter, which is the seat of the operation of chemical action, we are able to go a good way back by actual experiment; and even when we have gone as far back as experiment can carry us, or rather as far as we have hitherto been able to go by its assistance, a vista opens before us of a possible explanation extending much further.

Here, then, on the one hand, in the construction of our organs of vision, and on the other, in the molecular constitution of matter and chemical combination, we have two instances of what is eminently conducive to our welfare, or even to our very existence, constituted as we are, which, in one respect, we may say, lie at opposite extremes. In the one case we have an exquisitely constructed apparatus, of the formation of which, by natural causes, we can give no account, and which, for anything we can perceive, might have been different or absent without disturbing the general course of nature in other respects; but which, at the same time, fulfils what is required of it in such an admirable manner that we are irresistibly impressed with the idea that it was designed for its object. In the other case, we find processes going on which are essential indeed to our life, but which at the same time affect the whole

system of nature, and which lead us back by probable inference to a state of things vastly more rudi-
mentary than what now prevails, and from which
we have not the least reason to believe that the
present system could have been evolved *merely* by the
operation of the natural causes which we find at
work, and without calling in the intervention of a
Power above what we call nature. It would be, as
it seems to me, highly presumptuous to say that the
laws of chemical combination were established in
order that the life of man might be carried on; the
benefit which man derives therefrom is only part of
a vast system pregnant with consequences. Confin-
ing ourselves to what our own minds can take in, we
should, I think, more readily regard the organism
as adapted to the environment than the inanimate
environment as designed for a future organism. We
cannot, however, follow the adaptation of the organism to the laws of chemical combination in the same
way that we can the construction of the eye, not
merely as regards the portion which acts as an
optical instrument, but even as regards that structure which comes into use after the formation of
images on the retina. For in the latter case careful
dissection, combined with microscopical examination,
lead to the discovery of a minute structure, the office
of which can hardly be doubtful; though how it is
that it discharges its functions is a thing not at

present understood. But in the former case we are concerned with chemical substances of so complex a nature—the substances, namely, that are contained in the food, and those by which they are changed in the process of digestion, and those again into which they are changed—that the various changes can only most imperfectly be followed. In this respect the adaptation of the organism to chemical changes makes some approach, as regards our knowledge, to the adaptation of the eye to the perception of colour. We are not able in this case to adduce the adaptation as evidence of design, because we do not know what the mode of adaptation is. We cannot, however, doubt that there is adaptation of some kind; and, considering the importance of the effects produced, we cannot reasonably doubt that that adaptation, whatever it may be, was designed for the end that it fulfils.

There is nothing that I know of to indicate that, in the past history of our earth, new chemical affinities which did not previously exist were called into being. Observe that I say "called into being," not "called into play"; for conditions of temperature, etc., may very well have existed at one time which prevented, and at another time which permitted, the actual exercise of affinities which existed all along. There is nothing in our examination of the crust of the earth to indicate that it may not

have been built up under the existing chemical
affinities, together with gravitation, the development
of heat by condensation, and so forth, from a remote
condition in which the matter that now forms it was
in a simpler, a diffuse, condition, and there is a good
deal to lead us to entertain such a view of its past
condition. A process of alteration such as this we
designate evolution.

We are thus led to the contemplation of evolution,
as a process that has been going on for ages which
carry us so far back into the vista of past time as to
be almost illimitable. There is nothing at all atheistic
in this. However far back we may go in our speculations, we are only carried to a point which we feel
cannot be our goal, if we want to explain everything
by evolution. Even if we speculate on the ultimate
unity of matter, and suppose that at one time it
existed in the state of separate atoms, all alike, more
elementary than the molecules, or even the atoms of
the chemist, endowed with combining affinities of an
intensity answering to their elementary nature, and
that from these atoms were formed by an evolutionary process the elements of the chemist, and
from these elements a variety of compounds, still the
question arises—Whence came this inconceivably vast
array of primordial atoms, bearing in their perfect
similarity to one another the character of "manufactured articles," and endowed with these intense

affinities of combination ? To this question science
can give no answer. But if we admit the existence
of a God, whom we regard as the first cause of all
that is, then we may look on the evolutionary process that we have been contemplating as His way,
or at least one of His ways, of working. And we
deem it evolutionary, because it is of a nature to be
followed by our own minds; because it belongs to
the domain of scientific inquiry; because it is a process in which the final results are conceivably deducible
from the initial conditions, though, of course, we do
not pretend that our investigations are so complete
that we can actually thus deduce them.

In the evolutionary progress that I have been
contemplating, I have confined myself to inorganic
nature, and indeed, in the main, to one particular
department of inorganic nature: that which relates
to the building up of substances from their elements,
or it may be from substances even more elementary
than any that are known to the chemist. The question now arises—Are we justified in assuming that
in the whole realm of nature—inorganic, organic, or
whatever it may be—no progress has been made, at
least since some indefinitely remote time, in which
we contemplate, perhaps, the present universe as
having been in the condition of a fiery nebula or
something of the kind, except by a purely evolutionary process—a process, accordingly, which it

belongs to the domain of science to investigate and explain, though we can hardly hope that our explanation will ever be complete?

If we admit the existence of a Supreme Will as the originator of all things, it would be absurd to deny to Him a power of which we are innately conscious as existing in ourselves. If, then, we refuse to admit that the Supreme Will may, even subsequently to some very remote time to which our evolutionary speculations carried us, have directly intervened in the course of nature, that He may have created a new thing in the earth, our refusal must rest either on induction, on extending to the past our inference from the present observed course of nature, or else on deduction, on drawing conclusions from what we believe of the character of God as to what He might, or might not, be supposed to have done in the past.

Little reliance can be placed on the argument from induction, since the whole time over which our observations extend is but as a drop in the ocean, compared with the vast periods of past time to the contemplation of which our researches lead us. The period over which accurate scientific observation has extended, especially anything like widespread observation, is but a small fraction of the time which has elapsed since the earliest historical records. To draw inferences as to the almost illimitable past from

10

such a speck of time as that over which accurate and
extensive scientific observation has extended, would
be hazardous in the extreme. And if, in order to
extend the time which we may refer to in framing
our induction, we include historical records of the
past, whether it be human history or the history
which is embedded in the rocks, the evidence cuts
both ways. In human history we read of wars, and
famines, and earthquakes, etc., just like things that
go on to the present day. But we also read of events
asserted to have taken place, which we cannot refer
to the operation of such natural causes as those which
we make the subject of scientific inquiry. In some
cases the evidence is not such as to lead us to believe
that the asserted events really occurred, and we
speak of the statements as myths or legends. But
in some cases the evidence is of so conclusive a
character, and the events themselves are so bound
up with a system of which they form a part, that
they have been accepted by millions and millions of
the most enlightened nations, and have influenced
the whole course of the lives of individuals, and the
policy of nations. Again, if we turn to the testimony of the rocks, we find remains of plants and
animals that have long since passed away, of
forms differing from one geological age to another,
yet, on the whole, exhibiting a sort of rough
order of sequence. What are we to think of these?

What are we to think of the origin of life itself upon our earth?

There are strong scientific reasons, into which I do not propose to enter, for believing that our earth was once in a condition of temperature utterly unfitted for the existence of living things, be they animals or plants, or at least of living things having the remotest resemblance to those with which alone we are acquainted. How, then, are we to suppose that life began upon earth? When the temperature was sufficiently reduced, are we to suppose that certain molecules came into chance collisions of such a kind that, somehow or other, a living thing was produced, having the wonderful property of reproducing a living thing similar to itself, and so on in indefinite generations? Well, the temperature of the earth is at the present day suited for the maintenance of the life of living things, both plants and animals, and if a living thing came into existence in time past by the chance collision of molecules, why should not the same thing take place now? Why should we not have the same thing occurring at least now and then? And, indeed, not so very long ago there were some who imagined that the phenomenon did occur, though even they did not assert it, except in the case of certain microscopic animalcules which were found in putrifying solutions. The best experimentalists have, however, now shown that the supposed origination of life from dead matter was due to defects in the experiment, so that now our best biologists admit that, so far as we know, life can only proceed from life. It would be wrong, however, I think, to regard the evidence as trembling in the balance—as awaiting the result of some extremely difficult experiments. The phenomena of life are so peculiar, so utterly unlike anything that we witness in lifeless matter, that it would require the very strongest experimental evidence to lead us to accept the possibility of spontaneous generation. I think that even very strongly pronounced evolutionists at the present day would, in general, admit that the commencement of life upon the earth required the exertion of a power above the ordinary laws of nature. This amounts to the admission of the exertion of creative energy, at a time separated, indeed, from the present by a series of geological ages, but yet long subsequent to what we look on as a still earlier stage in the history of our earth.

There is nothing in such an exertion of creative energy antagonistic to an evolutionary progress, in all other respects, of the earth itself. When man exerts his will, and brings about some change thereby, suppose the cutting down of a hill, the natural forces remain all through just as they were. Consequently the evidence of an evolutionary progress, extending from a time long anterior to the first appearance of life upon the earth, and continued as before after that appearance, does not in the least militate against the supposition of the exertion of a creative energy by which life was first originated upon earth.

But the existence of life upon earth is not the only thing we have to consider. There is a vast variety of different forms of life upon the earth at the present day, and the forms have changed from one geological age to another. What are we to think of all this? Are we bound to assume that each of those forms which we recognise as distinct was a separate and independent creation? Or are we to suppose that the whole came about by an evolutionary process, being derived from the primitive living germ?

I cannot perceive that we are in the slightest degree confined to these two alternatives. The similarity of neighbouring species of plants and animals, the general sequence of forms in past ages, seem to point to some sort of evolution; on the other hand, the wide differences between different types of living things seem to me to forbid the idea of the whole having come by an evolutionary process from a single form.

Some, it may be, look on evolution simply as God's mode of working, and would object to draw a distinction between evolution and an exertion of creative power, unless, perhaps, with reference to the first commencement of life upon the earth. This view does not dispense with a Creator, nay, it regards Him as the continual sustainer of the universe. It involves, however, an induction which rests, as I think, on quite too narrow a basis. From what we can observe in the very limited time over which our observations extend, it assumes that God's action in the past was limited to those gradual changes, taking place according to previously existing laws, to which the term "evolution" is more commonly applied; that there was nothing analogous to changes brought about by the direct action of our own wills. This is, I think, to go quite beyond what the evidence justifies. What we actually observe of the course of nature leads us naturally to suppose that, if changes were brought about in the past in a way transcending that which has just been described, such deviations from the usual course of nature were rare, and are not to be rashly assumed. For my own part, I prefer to retain the distinction between evolution and the exertion of a creative power, using the former term in the narrower, and, I think, more usual sense; but, as to the latter, I refrain from any speculation as to the mode of exertion.

But it may perhaps be said to me, What do you consider to be referable to an evolutionary process, and where do you suppose that a creative energy was exerted? My reply must be, This is a question

which you should put to a biologist, not to me.   At
the same time I must frankly say that, try whom
you will, I do not think you will get a satisfactory
answer.   I do not think that it is a question that
science can answer; but, at the same time, I do not
think it is one with the answer to which theism is
concerned.

I must, however, so far qualify this last statement
as to say that I think there is one point at which
theology at least, though not perhaps theism, is concerned with the reply that may be given.   Are we to
look on man as having come by evolution, by some
slow condition of change from some lower animal,
or are we to suppose that he was created by a special
exertion of Divine energy, no matter whether his
body was formed of lifeless matter, which was then
endowed with life and intelligence, or an intellectual
and moral nature was superadded to an animal
nature previously existing, his bodily structure being
modified in accordance with his raised position ?   Or,
to state the question briefly, and without introduc-
ing subordinate and apparently immaterial matters,
was he a special creation ?

Now surely there is such a gulf between the
intellectual and moral nature of man, and the mind
of even the most intelligent of the lower animals,
that, unless we are prepared to give up all intervention of creative power in the world of life, this must

be one of the points at which we must suppose it to have been exerted.

The homologies which exist between the bodily structure of man and that of other mammals do not affect the argument. Mental characters are not a thing to be made out by the skilful use of the knife and the microscope; and if the resemblance between the bodily structure of man and other mammals had been far greater than it is, that would have left the argument intact. It could only have affected it on the supposition that a demand was made that man's body should be framed *directly* from inorganic materials; and even then, the similarity of bodily wants might be supposed to require a general similarity of bodily structure. But there is no need to introduce purely adventitious questions of this nature. If it be admitted that in the origination of man something more was required than a mere evolutionary process taking place under the operation of those laws which it is open to the scientist to investigate, we need not further concern ourselves with the mode of origination.

I am aware, of course, that those who hold an evolutionary origin of man would, as regards his mental capacities, look rather to real or supposed resemblances between his mind and the minds of lower animals, especially the more intelligent, than to the resemblance of bodily structure. But without

denying that lower animals have minds of some kind,
and are even, it may be, to some slight degree capable
of reasoning, we have no evidence that I know of
that shows that they have a conscience, or that they
are capable of that apparently unlimited power of
carrying on a chain of reasoning, which is the pre-
rogative of man.

The deductive argument to which I referred
against the supposition of the exertion *in time* of
a creative energy will not require any lengthened
notice.   There are some evolutionists who, while
theistic, seem to look on it as derogatory to the
character of God to suppose that He exerted creative
energy from time to time.   It is, they would say, as
if the world, as it came from His hands, were so
imperfect that it required, so to speak, to be patched
up from time to time.

But the creative acts which we have been
supposing do not involve a breaking up of what
previously existed, a dereliction of any of the laws
of nature which were previously in existence, and
the substitution of new ones.   The change is of
the nature of an addition to the kosmos that
previously existed of a structure beneficently
designed, amenable to the previous natural laws,
which remained intact, but having besides laws of
its own, which were superadded to the former.
Suppose that the earth cooled down in the course

of ages from a fiery state, until at last its condition became comparable with that which it has at present. What is there derogatory to our idea of God in supposing that when the fulness of time was come, when the earth that had for ages been in preparation had attained a suitable condition, then the creative power was exerted, and living things brought into being; or even that afterwards, as the condition of the earth was gradually matured, other forms, suitable to the new condition, were similarly created? Why should it be thought to be more agreeable to a proper idea of God to suppose that the earth and all its furniture were potentially involved in a fiery nebula, so that its molecules, by virtue merely of the forces inherent in them, after they had come together and formed a world, presently settled themselves down into living things of various forms, changing from one kind to another in the course of subsequent ages? Do we exalt our ideas of the Almighty by assimilating Him to the gods of the Epicureans, who created the world, and then left it all to itself?

Of course, we are not needlessly to bring in the supposition of creation in order to explain a phenomenon for which we do not see at once any mode of accounting. The ordinary course of nature proceeds according to fixed, definite laws, which man gradually comes to find out, and then he can avail himself of his knowledge of those laws to make his arrangements in accordance with his wants. When a strange phenomenon is presented, be it in the material records of the past or in any other way, we are not at once to refer it to a cause above the ordinary course of nature. Let science do her best to explain it if she can. But if, after all her endeavours, no progress has been made or seems possible, and the phenomenon itself does not even seem to be akin to others which have been explained, then we should not rule out of court the supposition that it may have been brought about by a creative act.

I have treated the question of successive creations as one bearing on the most reasonable account of observed phenomena. But it is but fair that I should not conceal my belief that the acceptance or rejection of the idea of successive creative acts has very important theological bearings. If, in spite of the enormous difficulty, amounting almost to an apparent impossibility, of explaining the records of the past by reference to merely the ordinary natural laws, we absolutely reject the idea of the exertion of a creative power, it seems hard to believe in anything which is professedly supernatural; and with the rejection of the supernatural must go any religious system in which the supernatural is involved; or, at least, such ideas of the character of God, and

such motives for action as are founded on the acceptance of what is asserted to have taken place in a
manner transcending the ordinary course of nature
are taken away, and what may be saved from the
wreck must suffer in reputation, and in its claims
upon our acceptance, from having been associated
with what can only be regarded as either a delusion
or a fraud.

Before taking leave of you for the present, it
may be convenient to refer briefly to the subjects which I have brought before you in these
Lectures.

In opening my present course, I said I should
allow myself greater liberty than I had previously
done in dwelling on scientific matters, not, however,
in order to bring before you recent discoveries, or
things of purely scientific interest, but merely
results to which the pursuit of science had led, it
may be led long ago, and which were of a nature
to be turned to account in some way towards the
object of the Gifford Foundation. I said I did
not propose to multiply examples, for as regards
the ultimate object which I was bound to keep
in view, there would have been in that way much
duplication.

In my first Lecture I referred to the subject
of the luminiferous ether, which has only come

prominently into notice since the revival of the undulatory theory of light about the commencement of the present century. It pervades the whole visible universe, and yet our senses give us no direct cognisance of it. Its properties, so far as we know them, are in some respects altogether different from what we should have expected beforehand, and there is a great deal about them which is still mysterious. If even in the investigation of the properties of the ether, a thing which belongs to physical science, we should have been led astray, and should have missed great discoveries—if, presuming upon the supposed completeness of our knowledge, we had summarily rejected a hypothesis involving suppositions which seemed unlikely when judged of by means of our previous knowledge, how much more likely is it that we should make mistakes, and miss, it may be, some things highly important to our welfare, if, relying upon our knowledge of the laws of nature, we summarily dismissed the evidence of asserted facts, which, if true, are of a nature to lie altogether outside the ordinary course of nature.

In my second Lecture, following out the physical subject of the first, I showed how, by studying as best we can the properties of the mysterious ether, we were led to the *conception* of the instantaneous transmission of intelligence from one

part of the universe to another. Passing then to
a different subject, I pointed out how, in the
study of physical science, the simple and fundamental laws of motion do not suffice—or at least
we have no ground for saying that they do
suffice—for the explanation of phenomena. We
are obliged to add the attraction of gravitation,
resulting in phenomena perfectly obedient, indeed,
to the laws of motion, but which those laws alone
would not explain. In a similar manner, we are
obliged to regard magnetism as something superadded to the laws of motion and to the law of
gravitation, and so on, as regards other influences.
Passing then from inorganic nature to the world
of life, I pointed out how utterly distinct were
the phenomena of life from anything belonging to
the inorganic world, and how superficial were any
prima facie resemblances; indicating that in life
there was something superadded to the laws of lifeless
matter, to which, at the same time, it was obedient.
I stated that the best conception I could form of
such an influence was something of the nature of
a directing power, commanding, while not itself consisting of, ponderable matter. The existence of
such a thing is, of course, hypothetical; but to
suppose that in living things something of the
kind is superadded to the properties of dead
matter is perfectly analogous to our progress in

physical science, where we look on gravitation as
superadded to the laws of motion, magnetism as
superadded to both, and so on.   The materialistic
hypothesis is, that a living organism is merely a
highly elaborate machine constructed out of ponderable matter, obeying the laws belonging to ponderable
matter as such, *and nothing else,* but performing its
functions, even those of thinking and determining,
simply and solely as a machine, by virtue of its
construction.   I contrasted this hypothesis with a
non-materialistic view, such as that which I called
directionism, pointing out the inherent difficulties
of materialism apart from its tendencies, but also
referring to what seems to me to be its injurious
tendency in the direction of even natural theology,
as leading to fatalism, fostering an idea of irre-
sponsibility, and rendering difficult a belief in the
possibility of any living existence for man after
death, and thus conducting him towards pure
secularism.

In my third Lecture I selected for your consideration the organ of what is perhaps, in some respects,
the most wonderful of our senses—the sense of sight
—passing lightly over its construction as an optical
instrument, which is pretty familiarly known, and
going on to the commencement of the path which
leads from the affection of the organ by the external
agent to the mental sensation.   I dwelt on the

marvellously refined construction of that remarkable layer of the retina, called the "bacillary layer," so closely set in a necessarily definite order, and pointed out the requirements for single vision with the two eyes, and the way in which these requirements were provided for.

In my fourth Lecture I dwelt on the evidence of design which these wonderful structures evince, and then invited your attention to the beauty of the markings and colours of various creatures, and the inference we should naturally be disposed to draw from them, that they were designed to be enjoyed by man, and probably creatures lower in the scale.

In my fifth Lecture I dwelt on the molecular constitution of ponderable matter, and the formation of more complex from more simple kinds of matter, by chemical combination. The latter may conceivably have been deduced from the former by an evolutionary process. Not only so, but we may conceive of the simplest bodies with which chemists are acquainted as having themselves been formed in a similar way from matter in forms yet more elementary than any that chemists have attained to, perhaps even from some one primordial form. These speculations give the freest scope to an evolutionary process which leads to results of the highest importance to our welfare.

Lastly, in my Lecture to-day I have endeavoured

to point out that there is no incompatibility between
an evolutionary process extending over ages and the
superposition thereto of occasional creative acts for
special purposes. Our observation of the usual uni-
formity of nature warrants us in declining to refer
observed phenomena to such an origin, so long as
there appears to be a reasonable prospect of attributing them to the ordinary operation of what we
call the laws of nature, but it does not warrant us in
giving an unlimited extension, in time and range, to
evolution; in other words, in pronouncing the whole
of the phenomena which meet us in our study of
nature certainly to lie within the domain of science
to investigate and explain. I need not recapitulate
what I have just said as to certain moral consequences which, as it seems to me, arise from the
adoption of the one or the other of these two views.

    With these remarks I will close the present instal-
ment of my second course of Lectures. My duties
in my own university demand now my presence
there. I hope, however, to be here again about eight
weeks hence, and to deliver a few more Lectures
before the classes in this university separate.

    In the Lectures which I close to-day, I have en-
deavoured to bring before your notice some scientific
subjects in greater detail than I ventured to do in
my first course. I have had no novelties wherewith
to interest those of my audience who have already a

                           11

fair acquaintance with science. As I said in opening
the present course, I should not feel at liberty to
bring scientific matters before you unless it were
such as could in some way be turned to account in
promoting the object of the Founder; and much that
I have mentioned is so trite and well known, that I
fear I may have been wearisome to the scientific
portion of my hearers. Others, on the contrary,
may possibly have had a difficulty in following the
brief references to scientific matters which I have
made. The applications which I have been able to
make to natural theology, which is the Lecturer's
proper subject, are less direct and copious than I
should have wished. Still it is possible that some
things that I have said may have started trains of
thought in your own minds, which, perhaps, might
not have occurred to you before. It only remains
for me now to thank you for the attention with
which you have listened to me, and to express the
wish I feel that what I have said had been better
worthy of it, and more conducive towards the fulfilment of the ideal conception of the Founder of these
Lectures.

LECTURE VII

Introduction of some points belonging to the Christian religion—
Natural condition of man—Was his origin special, or wholly
evolutionary ?—Theological difficulties which beset the latter
supposition removed by the former—Bearing of the two on the
possibility and origin of a future life—Question of the original
condition of man supposing his origin special—The supposition
of his fall from a primal condition of innocence removes various
difficulties—Desiderata left by merely natural theology.

AT the commencement of my present course of Lectures, I expressed the intention of allowing myself
greater freedom than I had done in my first course,
both in the way of entering more fully into some
scientific matters, provided they bore in some way
on the object of the Gifford Foundation, and also in
mentioning some points of Christian teaching. In
the first instalment of the present course I dwelt at
some length on questions of science. In my remaining Lectures, I propose to refer with greater freedom
than I have hitherto done to some points belonging
to the Christian religion.

It might be supposed that materials towards the
formation of a methodical science of natural theology,

answering to the ideal conception of Lord Gifford, might be obtainable by means of a comparative study of the various religions of the world, both ancient and modern, existing among nations of various degrees of civilisation down to the lowest savages. Be that as it may, it is a task for which I feel myself wholly incompetent, and I shall not attempt it.

But there is one religion, professed in somewhat modified forms by the most civilised nations in the world, with which we are more nearly concerned; and if there be any religion to which the Lecturer is at liberty to refer, surely he cannot be debarred from mentioning this. It is true that it is founded upon what, at least, professes to be a revelation; and that, in Lord Gifford's Will, the wish is expressed that the Lecturers should treat their subject "without reference to, or reliance upon, any supposed special exceptional or so-called miraculous revelation." But taking into account the whole of the context, I think it is clear that what they are forbidden to do, is to *found* their conclusions upon revelation; they must get on as well as they can without that. In fact, a system of theology *founded* upon what professes to be a revelation would no longer be *natural* theology. But I cannot think that it could have been intended by the words, "without reference to" any revelation, to exclude even any mention of what may be supposed to have been revealed. I shall accordingly hold myself free to "refer" in this sense to what is generally believed to have been revealed, and to inquire whether it appears to fall in with what, by our natural powers, we feel to be right and just and good; whether it is in any way opposed to the well-established conclusions of science; or whether, on the contrary, its teaching is analogous to what we learn about natural things in the pursuit of science.

The most distinctive feature of this religion is implied in its name. But as mankind lived upon the earth thousands of years before the coming of Christ, it appears reasonable to examine, in the first instance, their natural condition. But in the expression "natural condition," I should wish to include, not merely the condition of man as he is now, but also what we may suppose to have been his original condition. Perhaps it might be said, "Given that he is what he is, what does it matter for our purpose how he got there?" Directly, perhaps, it may not matter, yet indirectly I think that it will be found that a great deal turns upon it. This brings us face to face with the question of the origin of man. Did he come into being by a purely evolutionary process —by slow continuous variation from some form of life which was not man at all? or was a moral and intellectual nature superposed on matter previously destitute of those qualities, be it that that matter was previously living, or that, having been previously destitute of life, life was conferred upon it, of a kind combining the attributes of an animal and of a spiritual being ?

In the revulsion from the old notion that each species of animal or plant, with possible exceptions in the case of some very closely allied, was an independent creation, the hypothesis of evolution has, at the present day, been carried to very great lengths. This is what constantly happens in the recoil from a position which is believed to be unsound, and it is perhaps conducive to the common weal that it should be so.   The difference of opinion stimulates inquiry, which may, in the end, be conducive to the discovery of the truth; and if those who range themselves on the one side or the other may possibly be somewhat biassed towards their own opinions, the public at large have, at least, the benefit of hearing the counsel on both sides.   The foremost biologists allow that, so far as we know, or have reason to believe, life can come only from life; and some even strongly pronounced evolutionists would seek something beyond evolution for the origin of man upon earth.   In fact, the strongest reason for assuming an evolutionary origin is the analogy of his bodily construction to that of other mammals, and this leaves untouched the question of his mental powers, which, after all, form the most marked distinction between him and the lower animals.   Observation can go but a very

little way towards tracing any such connection
between the mind of man and that of any of the
lower animals as an evolutionary origin would seem
to demand. And as to the analogy of bodily structure, which forms the strongest argument for a purely
evolutionary origin, that may be accounted for on
the supposition of a special creation in either of two
ways. In the first place, we may suppose that the
mental powers of man were conferred upon some
previously existing animal form, without more alteration of bodily structure than was compatible with
some sort of evolutionary bodily change—a supposition as much requiring a creative power as if man
had been formed directly from materials not endowed
with life. On this hypothesis all that evolution
demands would be granted to it, so long as we confine ourselves to bodily structure, beyond which the
argument for an evolutionary origin can hardly go.
In the second place, if we suppose that man was a
special creation as regards his bodily structure, as
well as in relation to his mental endowments—that
he was formed, it may be even directly, from materials not endowed with life—still the similarity of his
bodily wants to those of other animals might demand
a general similarity of structure, if he were not
merely to be capable of living, but to be, as the
lower animals are, well fitted for the kind of life
that he was to lead.

Seeing, then, that the supposition of a special creation of man, to the extent at least to which alone we are concerned with it from a theological point of view, is not inconsistent with such arguments as can be brought to bear in favour of a purely evolutionary origin, we may at least assume it as a working hypothesis, and examine whether the hypothesis affords any solution of certain moral problems which otherwise present much difficulty. And if the possibility of thus obtaining a solution, even partial, should lend some additional evidence to the hypothesis, we are not authorised to reject it on the ground that it is of a nature wholly different from that by which propositions in natural science are established, or made highly probable. For the very argument which has been used in favour of the hypothesis of a special creation is one depending on moral, not physical, considerations; and therefore it might be expected that the evidence for or against the truth of the hypothesis should be of a moral rather than a physical nature.

The supposition that man was in some way specially created relieves us from a formidable difficulty with which the hypothesis of a purely evolutionary origin is beset—beset at least unless we are prepared to throw Christianity overboard altogether, and adopt a creed of mere secularism, notwithstanding the difficulties which the supposition that the present

life is man's all presents to even natural theology.
For if there be a living existence of any kind for
man after death, the supposition that survival of
any kind is confined to the human race would involve a change of condition which takes place *per
saltum* as we pass continuously from the lower
animals to man; and a change of this kind is contrary to the notion of a purely evolutionary origin.
If we admit a future life for man, we must, on the
purely evolutionary hypothesis, be prepared to make
the same admission for man's companion, the faithful
dog; nor can we stop there, for surely there is more
difference, when we take the entire nature, and not
mere bodily structure into account, between man
and the lower animals than between, say, a dog and
some other species; between that again and some
third species, and so on. In short, we can find no
halting-place so long as we adhere to the hypothesis
of a continuous and purely evolutionary transmuta-
tion. I think the extravagance of such a conclusion
would tend very strongly to undermine all belief
in a future state, and lead to the adoption of the
secularist creed, whether openly avowed or secretly
entertained.

But if we admit the unique character of man
among animals when his whole nature, and not
merely his bodily frame, is taken into account, it
stands to reason that if there be a living existence

for him beyond the grave, it is to be sought for, not in connection with those things which he has in common with the lower animals, but rather in connection with that spiritual side of his nature, in regard to which he stands alone in the animal kingdom. It is something accordingly lying altogether outside that kind of evolution which we contemplate in the pursuit of natural science; something lying outside evolution altogether unless we give an extended signification to the word, and use it to include a sort of spiritual evolution; something lying outside the domain of natural science, though possibly the sort of evolution which we study in natural science may afford useful hints by way of analogy in relation to this evolution (if such we may call it) of a higher type.

If now, relieved by the frank recognition of man's unique nature from the necessity of either denying a living existence to man after death, or sharing it with some at least of the lower animals, we seek to inquire after the evidence of such an existence and its conditions, we are at once turned away from those things in relation to man with which natural science is concerned, and directed to man's intellectual or spiritual nature.

If death be not the termination of man's living existence, evidence of survival might conceivably be derivable either (1) from a chain of reasoning of a

purely intellectual character, or (2) from a sort of
instinct, or (3) from an almost instinctive feeling
that some sort of retribution is required to accord
with the belief we have of the equity of the Ruler
of the universe, or (4) from a communication made
to man in some supernatural way, the evidence that
it was so made lying of course within his natural
powers (taking this expression in its most general
sense) to judge of.

(1) Some have professed to establish man's survival of death, and even to prove him to be immortal,
by metaphysical arguments founded on the supposed
nature of the soul. To my own mind all such arguments appear to be absolutely worthless. To me
the familiar fact that in profound sleep or in a faint
time elapses, and yet thought is in abeyance, affords
conclusive proof that a survival of death is not to
be established (speaking for myself, I would say, nor
even made probable) by any such *à priori* arguments,
and apart from all moral or religious considerations.
Observe I am not saying for a moment that the
familiar phenomena of sleep or a faint are inconsistent with the supposition of the survival of death,
but only that (to my own mind at least) they de-
molish any metaphysical argument for survival
founded on the nature of the soul itself. For if
thought may be in abeyance for five minutes or five
hours, it may equally well be supposed to be in

abeyance for five years, or five million years, or for
ever.   In other words, so far as anything founded
merely on the nature of thought can show, death
might be an eternal sleep.

(2) In our ordinary lives we go on thinking, and
we fully expect to continue our thoughts the next
moment, and so on.   Perhaps, if it were not for
experience, we might have a difficulty in conceiving
the possibility of its being otherwise.   Perhaps, if
we saw in another person the outward manifestations of thought cease at the moment of his death,
we might have assumed as a matter of course that
he was thinking still, though about what we could
not tell.   But we *have* experience to guide us.
When a faint is coming on we go on thinking, and
do not anticipate any cessation of the process.   Or,
at least, if we do, it is not any instinctive expectation, but a reasoning from past experience as to
what may probably be the result.   But the absence
of any instinctive expectation of a cessation of
thought does not defend us from it; and when we
come to, the change in our surroundings shows us
that time has elapsed, though we knew nothing of
it.   The same thing is shown, not indeed so clearly
and sharply, but in a way of which everybody has
had experience, in ordinary sleep.   Experience then
shows how little reliance, as an argument for the
survival of death, can be placed on our ordinary

expectation of the continuation of thought from
moment to moment.

(3) The feeling of right and wrong is too general
in the human mind to be attributable merely to the
result of education, though, of course, it admits of
development under proper instruction. I should
suppose that the feeling that right and wrong
actions demand requital forms one of the strongest
reasons, apart from revelation, for supposing that
this life is not man's all, though on this point I
cannot speak with any authority, not having made
a study of the various religions in the world. Be
that as it may, we see from the writings that have
come down to us that men of acute and cultured
mind did not get further than to entertain a more
or less probable belief in a future life; and it seems
evident that man merely by the exercise of his
natural faculties cannot arrive at a knowledge of
the duration or conditions of a future life, if such
there be; or, at least, can only gain a general idea
that it would in some way or other afford opportunity for retribution according to deserts, the
necessity for which formed one of the chief reasons
for believing that there would be a future life at all.

(4) It is a matter of notoriety that the existence
of a future life forms part of the Christian religion,
and is involved in what is believed to be a revelation come from God. Into this I may not enter

further than to say that if man by his natural powers can get no further than to have strong suspicions that there may be a life beyond, and can make out nothing, or next to nothing, of its conditions, if there be such a life, it stands to reason that if he rests his belief of it on what he holds to be a revelation, he should approach the study of that revelation with an open, unbiassed mind, ready to be taught what may there be found as to the conditions of the future life.

The purely evolutionary theory of the origin of man, as distinguished from that of a special commencement, leads to a conclusion as to man's duty which it may be well to mention, though I doubt if it has ever been pushed to such a conclusion.

In the animal world we find a variety of species admirably adapted for attack as well as for defence, and they employ ruthlessly the weapons with which they are furnished against the animals on which they prey, or even in some cases with which they fight, though, perhaps, without the necessity of preying upon them. Frequently fierce battles take place even between animals of the same species, while in other cases they herd together and assist one another in the common battle against animals of a different species—as, for example, in the case of wolves, which hunt in packs. Animals of the same family may assist one another—as, for example, a lion and lioness and their cubs; and in the case of gregarious animals, something of the same kind may exist between different members of the same herd. But towards animals of a different species, especially when they are preyed upon, and to some extent even as regards animals of the same species, the general rule appears to be, each one for himself.

Now the theist is bound to suppose that, on the whole, this is conducive to the welfare of the animal kingdom. It is the arrangement which God has adopted, and there is no moral evil connected with it, for we have no reason to suppose that the lower animals are endowed with a conscience, or even that they are capable of regarding as cruel what man would be disposed to call by that name.

Now we can conceive an extreme evolutionist, who would deny any special origin for mankind, to point to the law of each for himself, which appears to reign in the animal world, and to argue, This is the plan which God has arranged for the whole animal world; but man, after all, is nothing but an animal, descended from some creature that we should not call man at all. Therefore the same law should apply to him. We should simply fall in with it. This reasoning might conceivably be used to justify even the sweating system, and things of a similar nature. I do not say that it is so used, and I should be sorry to be supposed to charge even extreme evolutionists with it. There is a voice within which condemns such an application. Yet for all that, I cannot help thinking that sound logic leads in that direction if we start with the premiss that mankind is an outcome of pure evolution.

I do not deny that the general law for the animal world, which we have been considering, has application within due limits even for man. Indiscriminate charity may do positive mischief; and man being what he is, he requires to be trained not a little in the stern school of necessity. But, holding as I do that man has a spiritual nature superadded to the animal, I would maintain that we cannot directly apply to the regulation of his conduct the laws which govern the mere animal world, but that these must be subordinated to the higher laws belonging to his higher nature.

What I have just been saying is rather a digression from the subject on which I began, and I return to a consideration of man's condition as connected with what we may suppose to have been his original condition, supposing that he had a special origin, and was not merely the outcome of a purely evolutionary process of change.

It is notorious that there is a voice within us declaring that such a course would be right and such a course wrong, and that we are far from invariably doing that which we feel to be right. Was it always so? I should think that a person who holds a purely evolutionary origin of man could hardly give other than an affirmative answer. But this involves a great moral difficulty, on which I will not dwell at length, as I have already mentioned it in my first course of Gifford Lectures. Briefly, it is that it represents sin as natural; in other words, as part of the regular constitution of nature as God made it—that it makes Him accordingly the Author of sin.

But if we adopt the alternative theory of man's origin—namely, that he had in some way a special beginning, be it only by the superaddition on some previously existing stock of that which is peculiar in his moral and intellectual nature—we are relieved from the great moral difficulty which I have referred to, because we are now no longer compelled to suppose that his present condition represents what his condition was when he came from the hands of his Maker. It may be that a change for the worse has come over him; a change the possibility of which seems to be necessarily involved in his possession of free will; a change which, once incurred, may have been communicated to his posterity in accordance with the laws of heredity. I need hardly mention that this supposition is in accordance with

12

certain statements which most Christians regard as authoritative.

But there are still further difficulties belonging to natural theology, of which we find a possible solution, if we may suppose that the present discrepancy between what a man ought to do, and what he too frequently does, formed no part of his original constitution.

How comes it that while man's mental powers seem to be adapted to indefinite progress, and that he aspires after continual advance, yet seldom fourscore years elapse ere death comes, and, to all outward appearance, makes an end of him altogether? Were those powers and those aspirations given him in mockery, as it were, only to be a source of disappointment? Or may we suppose that this discrepancy between his aspirations and the fate which lies before him did not belong to his original condition; that he was not designed to be thus cut off by death?

It may be said, Death reigns throughout the whole animal kingdom. Nor is this a thing of yesterday. The records of the rocks show that it was the same in past geological ages. How can we suppose that man, animal as he is, ever formed an exception to this general rule?

This argument would doubtless be immensely strong if we supposed that man took his origin by

a purely evolutionary process. But if we suppose
that man originated, whether wholly or only in part,
in a creative act, then, on account of his unique
nature, we are not authorised to extend to him the
induction founded on the observation of what befalls
the lower animals, as we should otherwise have done
without hesitation. It may be that the change we
have been supposing, whereby he broke through the
law of duty—a law which thenceforth became power-
less to preserve him in the path of uniform rectitude—
entailed a forfeiture of the exemption which he previously possessed from the fate of the lower animals,
and that thenceforth he became liable to have his
career cut off by death.

What man's condition, and what his destiny
might have been, if that primal condition of rectitude which we have been supposing had lasted, it
is useless now to speculate. That condition, if such
there were, having passed away, the speculation
would be unpractical, a mere matter of curiosity;
and neither reason nor revelation affords us an
answer.

The supposition of the special origin of man,
accordingly, if it may be entertained, relieves us of
certain moral and teleological difficulties belonging
to the subject of natural theology, which are by no
means of trifling weight. It is one which, from
the very nature of the case, lies outside natural

science, and therefore the two cannot come into collision unless we start with the assumption that evolution (using the term in the restricted sense which I explained in a former Lecture) is at least theoretically sufficient for accounting for the whole nature of man. I need hardly say that our supposition is in accordance with certain statements which are usually regarded by Christians as possessing authority. If the contrary supposition presents serious difficulties in the way of even natural theology, the difficulties, as it seems to me, are still more serious in relation to Christianity. It is not as if it were merely a question of referring some isolated statement to an unauthentic tradition handed down in some very ancient Jewish writings—a statement which might be detached while leaving the rest intact. On the contrary, the special origin of man seems to be in several ways interwoven with the Christian system. It would be out of place to argue the question on the basis of what is held to be a revelation, but I surely am at liberty to refer to what is most commonly believed by Christians; to point out how the supposition of its truth relieves us of certain difficulties even independent of Christianity, and to ask what natural science has to set against it.

Now the only thing that natural science has to set against the supposition of a special origin for man is the assumption of the omnipotence of evolution for the explanation of natural phenomena. When I say "omnipotence," I ought, perhaps, to except the question of the origin of life; for several persons who, in other respects, go in completely for evolution, allow that, in this case, something more is required. Those who would extend evolution even to the origin of life must be prepared to face the enormous difficulties which beset every attempt to account for its origin by natural causes from mere lifeless matter, and the negative conclusions to which the best experimentalists have been conducted in the examination of the hypothesis of abiogenesis. Those who admit that, in this case, something more is required, have conceded a principle which possibly may have other applications, and which, therefore, cannot be rejected with a high hand, if, in some other case or cases, there should appear to be weighty reasons for having recourse to it.

But there is a second supposition which needs to be combined with that of a special origin of man, if we would solve the teleological difficulty which arises from the contrast between his capacities for, and aspirations after, continued progress, and the stop which, to all outward appearance at least, death puts to what he might have gone on to. To this second supposition, indeed, I have already alluded. It is that man's original moral condition was not such as

it is now; that it was one of innocence, free from
the upbraidings of conscience for wrong things done,
and from the accompanying alienation from his
Maker; and that it was in consequence of his fall
from that condition that he became liable to death,
for which otherwise he was not intended.

The supposition that man's original moral condition was not like his present, but was one of innocence, relieves us of a further teleological difficulty.
The upbraidings of conscience for doing wrong are a
source of pain; and if sin were part of man's original
nature, we have the enigma to solve, Why was that
which was natural to him made painful? I would
not, however, lay much stress on this difficulty,
because we have the analogy of bodily pain for
which a beneficent object may be suggested. Were
it not for the fear of the pain that would thence
arise, men and animals generally might wound or
maim themselves, and thus render themselves unfitted to take their proper part in life, or even destroy
themselves altogether. In a similar manner, it might
be said that the mental pain which results from doing
wrong was designed to keep men from wrong actions.

To sum up briefly what we have been considering,
so far as unaided natural theology can go, man's
actual condition must be regarded as his natural
condition, by which is meant the condition for which
he was fitted by his original constitution. Thus

regarded, his condition, taken in connection with our ideas of the character of God, presents various anomalies, which we are left to explain as best we can. The existence of sin, be it more or be it less, we find to be general, and the consciousness of it mars our happiness. As to any amelioration of this distress, all the hopes of moral improvement that natural theology can hold out to us are that, if we put out our utmost strength in striving after that which we feel to be right, we may gradually improve. Yet the prospect is not altogether encouraging. We find our endeavours are far from being always successful. Perhaps we might imagine that, if we had an unlimited time before us, we might slowly attain to a condition approaching indefinitely to perfect rectitude as a curve approaches its asymptote. But before a great many years are out death comes and puts a stop to any such progress, so far, at least, as we are able to follow; for what, if anything, lies beyond? As far as physical evidence goes we should say nothing. Moral considerations may lead to a supposition that there may be something beyond. But, after all, I think it must be confessed that, as far as man can make out by the exercise of his own unaided powers, death must be looked on in the main as a leap in the dark.

Though Christianity was engrafted on the Jewish religion, and though the existence of a life beyond the grave forms a cardinal point of it, it is remarkable how little reference there is to a future state in the Jewish writings before the Captivity. It would almost seem, from the records of the past, as if the Egyptians thought more about it in those days than the Jews, at least, if we take the rank and file of both nations. Does it follow from this that they were in a more advanced religious state? We might, perhaps, think so (supposing the fact to be as I have suggested) if the future state was a thing to be made out by man's unaided powers. But if the evidence of it be based on a revelation made from God to man, and *that* (at least in its fulness) not till thousands of years had passed, it is quite conceivable that, when made, its reception may have been easier to those who had not previously to unlearn teaching which, though it might contain some glimmerings of truth, was based on an erroneous foundation.

In matters of ordinary study—say, for example, in the study of natural science—there is an advance of knowledge in the individual, and an advance of knowledge in the race. The youth grows up and receives instruction from his seniors, but there are many things which he cannot take in until he has made considerably further progress. The stock of knowledge which is the possession of mankind is gradually added to through the labours of individuals ; and things, which at one age of the world could not be understood if they had been mentioned, are at a later stage readily taken in and assimilated. Now we can see no reason, *à priori*, why it should be different with regard to moral and religious advancement, so far at least as that knowledge is to be obtained simply by the exercise of man's unaided powers.

This leads up to the point for which I introduced this subject. Suppose it be asserted that there are important religious truths which lie altogether outside anything that man could discover by the exercise of his natural powers, however strenuously he might exert them ; that, accordingly, he must remain in ignorance of them, and destitute of the beneficial influence, if such there be, which they might exert on his character, unless a communication be made to him by some means lying above his natural power ; that such a communication has, in fact, been made to him ; have we any right to say that, if such a communication were made, it would have been made from the beginning, or at least as soon as the change took place from what we have been supposing to have been man's original condition ; that so long a postponement of such a communication does not accord with our ideas of the goodness of God ?

But may there not have been just the same sort of education needful for the race, in order to prepare them for the reception of the communication when it came, and for profiting by it, that there is in matters of ordinary human learning? If so, that would lead us to look into the condition of man as he is, independently of any such teaching; to consider the contrast between his aspirations and his actual condition; to inquire what prospect there is of those aspirations being fulfilled.

In the first place, there is a law written on the heart of man which tells him that such and such things are right, and, on the other hand, that such and such things are wrong. He feels the pain of self-condemnation when he does wrong, and yet he is not morally strong enough always to avoid it. I need not repeat what I said only a little while ago as to the imperfection of the fulfilment of his aspirations in this respect, and consequently the imperfection of his happiness, an imperfect fulfilment being the very utmost that he can hope to attain to by any such means as he can discover for himself.

In the next place, there are the aspirations after continued progress, which are rudely cut short by death; and as to the possibility of their being, in some way, carried on after death, man's unaided reason can but offer some vague conjectures.

Again, there is the unhappiness arising from pain and sickness. If it be said, this is only what belongs to man in common with the lower animals, to a certain extent no doubt that is true, and yet there is one not unimportant difference. So far as we know, or have reason to believe, the lower animals do not anticipate evils to come. They enjoy their life as they have it, whereas, with man, the anticipation of coming ills is an element of discomfort not to be altogether neglected.

The Christian religion holds out a prospect of release from all these evils. The means whereby this is to be effected are such as never could have occurred to man's natural reason, and, if accepted, must be taken on evidence of a different nature. Nevertheless, man's natural powers have their proper part to play, and an examination of the reasonableness or otherwise of what professes to be taught from a source above man's reason can hardly be deemed altogether foreign to the subject of natural theology.

LECTURE VIII

I HAVE already said that I felt myself wholly incompetent to undertake a comparative study of the various religions which have been held by the various nations of the world, both in ancient and modern times, with a view to possibly obtaining some materials towards founding a science of natural theology. And it may be doubted whether, after all, any great good would come out of such a study. At any rate, there is one religion with which we are more especially concerned. It is notorious that, at present, and for centuries back, the most highly civilised nations have almost universally professed the Christian religion. It is true that there are considerable varieties in the

precise forms in which it is held, so much so that, in
extreme cases, those who hold different forms seem
hardly to recognise each other as holders of a common
religion. Nevertheless, there is a far deeper sub-
stratum of unity than appears on the surface, and if
we examine those things with respect to which a
very general agreement exists, it is probable *à priori*
that we shall find such a general accordance between
what is so held, and what commends itself to our
moral feelings, as almost to lead us to regard these
things as belonging to "natural theology," even
though, obvious as some things may appear when
we have been instructed in them, we should probably not have discovered them by the mere exercise of our natural powers; while, of course, there
are other portions of them which lie altogether
outside what man could have discovered, so as not
properly to fall within the province of natural
theology.

In any branch of knowledge it is often of importance, as preparing the way for the ultimate discovery
of the truth, to know when we do not know. For
example, the progress of the undulatory theory of
light, which is now supported by overwhelming
evidence, was at one time a good deal retarded by
predilections in favour of the corpuscular, notwithstanding its incompetence to link together the various
phenomena of light, including in particular the pheno-

mena of diffraction.   It belongs to true science. to
recognise the failure as well as the success of this
or that hypothesis which may have been put forward
to account for observed phenomena.

In a similar manner, in moral sciences, we are
called upon frankly to recognise the insufficiency, as
well as to accept the adequacy, according as the case
may be, of suggested solutions of the problems which
present themselves.

Just in the same way in the case of natural
theology, if problems meet us of which we can find
no satisfactory solution, it behoves us to recognise
that such is the fact.   It may be that a solution is
discoverable, though not yet discovered.   But it may
also be that a solution cannot be obtained at all by
human reason; and if we start with the assumption
that it can, that it lies within the province of natural
theology to find it, it may be that our assumption
is false, and may only lead us to spend, in vain, time
and thought that might have been turned to useful
account if we had sought for a solution in another
direction.   And it is conceivable that the effect
might even be worse, and that we should be led, not
merely to lose our time, but even to imagine that a
false solution was the true one, and thereby be put
off the track which might ultimately have led us to
the truth.

In my last Lecture, I referred to certain difficulties

which beset us if we would explain the actual condition of man, taken in conjunction with our ideas
of God, merely by the light of natural theology.
We have the anomaly of man's capacities for and
aspirations after continuous progress, and yet death,
so far as we can see, puts a stop to their operation
and fulfilment. We have the dissatisfaction arising
from doing wrong, and yet we do not uniformly do
right. We have the various ills that flesh is heir to,
which press far more heavily on man than on the
animal world in general, because his intelligence
enables him to anticipate these things beforehand,
and the discomfort thence arising is often worse
than the ills themselves when they do come, not to
mention that ills may be anticipated which never
come at all. Was man created for such things, or if,
though not created for them, he became subject to
them, is there no prospect of release ?

We know very well that the Christian religion
does hold out to us a prospect of the rectification of
these anomalies. But it is not through what is of
the nature of a scientific advance, made by the
mere exercise of man's natural powers. On the
contrary, the means by which it is to be brought
about are professedly supernatural; and it seems
almost axiomatic that what professes to be supernatural can only be attested by evidence which is
in part supernatural.

That which is supernatural cannot be based on mere natural theology. In relation to the supernatural, natural theology can but play the part of a bird in the nest, which opens its beak to take the food with which the parent bird supplies it, and digests what it thus obtains.

As to the opening of the beak, the question is simply—Are we authorised to reject what professes to be supernatural merely on the ground of its being such ? This question I have already discussed, and, therefore, I will not dwell on it further than to remark that even natural science presents us with problems for the solution of which we must have recourse to something above what it belongs to science to investigate; and that, not alone at some indefinitely remote time, but even after the state of things which now exists had made a considerable advance towards completion.

At the very basis of the Christian religion stands the belief that a revelation has been made from God to man through a Being in whom the two natures were united. How this union is effected is naturally a thing which lies beyond our powers to explain. When we contemplate the greatness of the system of the universe, the extent over the vast spaces and lengths of time which that contemplation leads us to conceive, and then, when we think of that as the work of a Supreme Being, it seems inconceivable to us how the Divine nature can be united with the finite nature of man. But although the mode of union is, as I said, a thing which altogether transcends our powers, we may, perhaps, be better able to form a conception of what is implied in the Christian idea by contemplating two conceptions, between which it lies.

Suppose that we know some specially good man, we feel the influence for good proceeding from him; we feel that he is above us, and yet is a man like ourselves; we know that his goodness is finite, and supposing him to be a human being, we know that that goodness is not perfect. Now, though we may exalt our ideas of such a good man by conceiving him to be free from those faults, however great or small, to which all of us are more or less subject, still the finiteness of his goodness remains, as the idea beyond which we cannot go. On the other hand, if we suppose the two natures united in the person of Christ, we may fall into the idea that the human nature belongs to the body, but that, as regards the mind, He partakes wholly of the nature of the invisible God, and is exempt from all the limitations which belong to the mental human nature of man.

Now the first of these conceptions stops short of the Christian idea; it limits our conception of the goodness of Christ to something comparable with,

13

and only more or less surpassing the goodness of
man; we do not, in this way, attain to the idea of
an absolute, infinite goodness. On the other hand,
if we think of Christ as man only as regards His
body, refusing to admit any other limitations such
as belong to human nature, we virtually deny His
true humanity; we lose the idea of sympathy with
us which the Christian conception of His true
humanity involves, and instead of contemplating
Deity through the veil of humanity we run the
risk of falling into a sort of Ditheism. The evidence
for a fact so astounding as that of the union of the
Divine and human natures in one Person does not,
of course, belong to natural theology, and to go into
Christian evidences would be foreign to the object
of the Gifford Foundation, further, at least, than to
examine whether our natural powers respond in any
way to what professes to be taught by supernatural
means. Though the mode of union is necessarily
above us, and we should never have dreamt of the
possibility of the two natures being thus united, we
can conceive what an enormous advantage such a
union, supposed to exist, is calculated to afford us
towards arriving at a knowledge of God, "Whom
truly to know"—I quote the very words of Lord
Gifford's Will, referring, of course, to the words of our
Lord—"Whom truly to know is life everlasting."

Though the law of duty is written on the heart,

still the blindness of man, connected as it is with
his derelictions of duty, led him often to mistake
what duty was, and to substitute for the performance of duty something which might pass for it, and
which would demand comparatively slight sacrifices.
In the accounts which have come down to us, we
see how frequently Christ swept away the cobwebs
of mere formal ordinances, and pointed out what
real duty was, in a manner which reached the hearts
of those who were not blinded by prejudice. The
common people heard Him gladly, but those who
would preserve their own ascendency on terms easy
to themselves, by passing off for duty the observance
of some merely formal ordinances, were exasperated.
Thus the unprejudiced natural judgment bore its
witness to the truth of His teaching. At the present
day there are many who, though unable to see their
way to assent to the supernatural bases of the
Christian system as a whole, yet recognise and
admire the loftiness of Christian morality. They
thus in their way bear their testimony, as far as it
goes, to the truth of the Christian system.

The feeling of the obligation of duty is natural to
man. It is a law written on the heart. But it is
one thing to feel what one ought to do and another
thing to do it. And in this last respect we are all
lamentably deficient. And this deficiency, and the
feeling of pain which belongs to it, constitute, as I

have already remarked, a teleological difficulty in
the way of natural theology.   The teleological
difficulty is removed, or, at least, so it seems to my
own mind, as I have already remarked, if we accept
in its broad outlines the account of man's origin
which is presented to us in what the generality of
Christians regard as authoritative.   But still the
question remains—Is there any hope that this conflict between duty and actual practice may be
brought to an end, so that a man shall never do
anything but what is right?   Now such a prospect
is held out to us in the Christian religion, not,
indeed, to be attained in the present stage of our
existence, though even here we should continually
tend towards it.   But the final attainment would
seem to involve something which we do not in our
present condition understand, but which is intimately connected with the death of Christ.
Attempts have, indeed, been made to give a
rationale of the whole, though, perhaps, it would
be more correct to say that the endeavours have
rather related to the avoidance of the full consequences of our misdeeds.   It may be doubted
whether such attempts may not, on the whole, have
done more harm than good.   In things which are
above us it is often best simply to say we do not
know, instead of offering explanations which will
not bear full examination.   Our inability to give

a full explanation of the *modus operandi* does not
debar us from being profited by the prospect. It
is not the part of a good child to refuse to believe
what his parents promise to do for him unless he
should fully understand in what manner it is going
to be done, or to refuse to obey their commands unless
he fully knows why the command was given.

But though the connection between the two
things is in the main above us, we get some glimpses
which show that it is not out of harmony with God's
government of the world as evinced by the ordinary
course of nature. It constantly happens that the
fault of one man brings suffering on another, or,
it may be, on a whole family. Sometimes the
sufferer has no option in the matter; but sometimes, also, a noble character will step in, and
voluntarily submit to toil or suffering in order to
avert the consequences which would otherwise have
followed from the fault of another person.

I have mentioned the teleological difficulty which
is presented by death in the case of the human race,
the difficulty arising from the circumstance that man
appears to be fitted for continued progress, and yet
his opportunities of progress are, at least to all outward appearance, cut short by death. Of course
natural theology might frame the hypothesis that
there is something in man which naturally survives
the stroke of death; but, then, natural theology must

largely depend on natural evidence, and the natural
evidence seems to be dead against it. I have mentioned how the teleological difficulty is removed—at
least, so it seems to my own mind—by the supposition that man's present moral condition does not
represent what it originally was; that he has fallen
from the original condition; and that, therefore, we
cannot argue from the actual and universal preval-
ence of death that man would have died had the
original condition been maintained.

The supposition of a fall from a primitive state of
innocence relieves us from the teleological difficulty
which I have mentioned. But it leaves our present
condition, so far as natural theology can inform us,
more hopeless than ever. For the only arguments
of any weight which natural theology has to offer in
favour of any survival of death for man are, as it
seems to me, half cut away. These arguments are
the teleological one arising from man's capacity for
continued progress, and the moral one arising from
our sense of the justice of the requital of right and
wrong, combined with our observation of the imperfection (at least as it appears to us) of such requital
in the present life. The teleological argument I may
say disappears, for the demands of the teleologist are
met by the supposition that man, in his original condition, was not designed for death; that his present condition, accordingly, is to be regarded as an

unnatural one, to which, therefore, we are not justified in applying the teleological argument. The
moral argument is, at the same time, robbed of
much of its force; for we might imagine that man's
fall from his original condition introduced a moral
confusion which constituted one of its disastrous
consequences.

It is notorious that the Christian religion pre-
eminently holds before us the prospect of a future
life; but it founds it, not upon a natural but upon
a supernatural basis—not on a conjectured natural
immortality of the soul, but on a promised future
resurrection, which it states to have actually taken
place already in the case of Christ Himself. As to
the condition of man in the interval between death
and resurrection, we may leave that as a subordinate
point, about which opinions may and do differ. It
is, I think, plain that, in the New Testament (which
surely we must take as the most authoritative exposi-
tion of Christian teaching), it is, at any rate in the
main, the resurrection state that is presented to our
view when a future life is referred to. Accordingly,
we are not confronted by embarrassments arising
from the observed connection between mind and
brain in the present life, rendering difficult, it may
be, to some the conception of human thought carried
on without any kind of organism; for it is distinctly
asserted that there is to be a future body, though

the nature and conditions of it are at present unknown.

If it were in connection with a fall from a primitive state of innocence that man became subject to death, it stands to reason, as at any rate most likely, that it would only be in connection with a restoration, in some way or other, to a state of continued innocence, that he would be introduced into a condition in which he would for the future be exempt from death. Such a condition the Christian religion does hold out before us—a condition of perfect rectitude—a condition of immortality.

Lastly, to take even bodily pain and sickness. These may often be useful as a corrective. They may, in particular cases, help in the education of a noble character. Yet, in themselves, they are no doubt an evil, and sometimes a very sore evil. From these, again, a prospect of release is held out to us.

We see, then, how the Christian religion, supposed to be true, satisfies man's highest aspirations; and how, at the same time, it affords solutions of what would otherwise appear to be perplexing anomalies. It involves much that, at present, we cannot understand, while, at the same time, different portions are found to be self-consistent, and consistent with things that belong to natural reason to judge of. As on a cloudy day, when the sky is mostly overcast, sunbeams here and there, passing through apertures in the veil of cloud, are seen illuminating the air, and pointing, it may be from a considerable distance, to a spot in the sky towards which they all converge, but which is itself invisible to us on account of the clouds; so this religion presents us with features which harmonise with one another, and with what we know in other ways, though the full blaze of truth towards which they all converge is still hidden from our view. If, in some respects, it strips away the rags with which mere natural theology endeavours to hide her deficiencies, it is to clothe her in a garment of surpassing beauty, in which she may modestly discharge the duties that belong to her proper sphere more efficiently than ever, while, at the same time, she is guarded from straying into a region that does not belong to her.

It might, perhaps, be objected to what I have been saying that I have treated man as an isolated individual, and have ignored his relations to others. In truth, this is only in appearance; for I have referred to duty, and a very large part of our duties has relation to our fellow-creatures. This branch of duty is one which appeals strongly to our natural sense of right and wrong, and is accordingly one which moralists have largely treated. It is needless to say how largely our duties to our fellow-men enter into Christ's teaching.

But it is not sufficient to know our duty. We might imagine that our whole range of duty was reduced to a system as accurate as a treatise on some branch of mathematics, and that we thoroughly apprehended it. We might still be very far from doing what we knew quite well we ought to do. If we fail to do what we ought to do, it is, I apprehend, far oftener from want of will than from want of knowledge; from being led away from what we know we ought to do by the desire of something else, or by the wish to escape the toil or suffering which the execution of the duty might bring with it. Against this, natural religion has to set the approval of conscience when we do what we feel to be right, and its condemnation when we do what we feel to be wrong. Besides this, there is a sort of instinctive feeling that wrong-doing must, in some way, bring evil in its train, I do not mean to the victims of the wrong, but to the wrong-doer; with this may be combined a feeling, perhaps somewhat less distinct, that the execution of what is right will, in the end, be for the advantage of the person who so acts. Yet we can hardly suppose that it was any considerations such as these that nerved men of old to noble deeds. When Regulus returned to Carthage to torture and to death, we cannot suppose that he was thinking of his future welfare. Rather we should imagine that he had made a firm resolve to follow the path of rectitude and honour, and the approval of his conscience was his reward.

Now I need hardly say that the Christian religion does not in any way weaken the voice of conscience, in approving or condemning what we do that is right or wrong; on the contrary, it allows that voice to be heard more clearly than ever, and extends it to acts and feelings that otherwise, perhaps, we might not have regarded. But, besides this, it holds out to us powerful motives for doing right and avoiding wrong, in respect to consequences to ourselves of the two courses of action—consequences, the general nature of which is indicated to us by natural religion, but which are presented to us in a clearer light than any that could be obtained merely from that source.

I have said that it is not sufficient for us to know our duty; for to know it is one thing, but to perform it is another. But I will now go further, and say that it is not sufficient for us to do our duty. It is conceivable (though I do not say that the conception is ever realised in actual practice) that a man should be led to do it simply and solely with a view to his own ultimate happiness. This, by itself, would be only a refined form of selfishness, or rather of mere self-interest. I use the latter term, because the word "selfishness" is generally taken to imply the disposition to do what is not merely for our own interest, but is for our own interest at the expense of the interest of somebody else, which would not be the idea I meant to convey. But if this stood by itself alone, there would be nothing in it incompatible with a hard unloving character, the possessor of which would be unworthy of being loved, though he might be respected for his firmness. Nor would such a character be conducive to the happiness of its possessor. In what he did he would be merely acting the part of a slave, doing right out of a sort of compulsion, not from the love of the right. He would not have the happiness which accompanies the enthusiastic pursuit of a worthy object; nor would there be any guarantee that he would continue in the same course of action if the pressure were removed.

All men are called on to work in one way or other; but there may be a great difference in the work done, and in the satisfaction or otherwise which the worker feels, according to the motives he has for doing the work.

First, take the case of a slave working under a harsh master. The slave, I will suppose, has no interest in the work, but he fears his master's lash if he neglects it. He works accordingly simply from the motive of fear, and he would fain escape from the thraldom he is under if he could. He has no interest in his work, and is content if it passes muster so that he escapes punishment.

Take, next, the case of an artisan who works for
wages. The work, perhaps, may not be very interesting, may even be monotonous, but he works of his
own free will, without compulsion, choosing, it may
be, the work in question in preference to some other
kind of work which would be less laborious, but would
not bring him as good wages. He feels that the
work is voluntary, and is content to go on with it for
the sake of the remuneration which he receives. He
takes probably some amount of interest in the work,
connecting it in his mind with the advantage which
it brings to him.

Lastly, take the case of a man who takes up some
piece of work, not for the sake of the reward it may
bring him (though, perhaps, there may be a reward),
but because his whole soul is in it, and he is most
anxious that it should be well accomplished. Work
done in this way is of the best kind, and, it is needless to observe, how much the happiness of the worker
is bound up with the doing of the work.

Now there may be similar motives urging us to
the performance of duty which is not imposed upon
us by an imperative necessity, but which our conscience tells us is a duty. First, there may be
the motive of fear of punishment for the neglect of
it. This may operate as a stimulant, but by itself
alone it does not seem to have any tendency towards
the creation of an amiable character; and, moreover,

the tendency of the human mind is to become callous under the long-continued influence of fear alone. Secondly, there is the hope of advantage to oneself to arise from the doing of the duty. This is so far superior to the former, as that it implies more or less of a feeling of attachment (perhaps love would be too strong a word) towards Him from whom the benefit is looked for. Yet in so far as it fails of this it hardly goes beyond a refined form of selfishness. Lastly, there is the motive of gratitude towards Him who enjoins the duty, and conformity of the human will to His will. This it is which produces enthusiasm in the work, and renders a man happy in the execution of it. Doubtless, all three motives are meant to have their influence, but a due proportion should be observed, and in the Christian religion the last and highest is brought out as in no other.

Of course, the case I was considering a little while ago—that of a man doing always what is right solely out of regard to his own interest—is a purely ideal one, both as to the supposed success in doing what is right, and in the absence of higher motives associated with those of mere self-interest. Still, its consideration may not be wholly useless, as tending to clear our ideas ; to show the insufficiency of motives of this kind standing by themselves ; to point out the error of supposing that this class of motives forms the staple of Christianity, as they are sometimes represented by opponents as doing; to point out the positive harm that may be done by exaggerating the personal consequences of courses of action, as is sometimes done by well-meaning persons, in the hope of frightening people into obedience, harm arising from the danger that considerations of this kind may usurp the place which ought to be left for higher motives, or may even act as an obstacle to their formation.

Now the Christian religion offers us encouragement in what, at first sight, would seem to be a strange way—namely, by setting before us a standard of duty which is nothing short of perfectness. This would seem to be absolutely unattainable, and the demand for it calculated to drive us to despair. And so it well might if we were left to our own strivings after it. And yet the prospect of ultimately attaining it—attaining, that is, a final delivery from sin—is actually held out to us, not, indeed, in the present stage of our existence, but in a life to come. But the attainment of this delivery is represented as involving a supernatural intervention arising out of the love of God for man, yet requiring at the same time that man should do his part, in the use of the means provided.

It may be well now to compare the prospect thus held out to us with the best that natural religion by itself alone has to offer.

As far as natural religion can inform us, the goal, involving as it does complete deliverance from sin, is one which we cannot hope to reach, but at the best only to approximate more and more nearly to. If we keep the ideal goal steadily before us, we cannot but be deeply sensible of how far we fall short of it, and can only look with despondency on the prospect. If, on the other hand, we look with complacency on the advances which we fancy we may have made, the satisfaction which we thence derive is at the expense of a virtual, if unavowed, lowering of the standard to be aimed at. Neither condition is conducive to a vigorous warfare.

On the other hand, the Christian religion holds out to us the prospect, nay, the assurance, of ultimate success if we continue always pressing onwards. It relieves us thus from the thraldom arising from a feeling of the hopelessness of the attainment of the object striven after, and prevents us from being unduly depressed and disheartened by our failures, by the wounds which we receive in the fight. At the same time, as the actual attainment of the object is represented as involving a gift from God to man, a gift to which he could lay no claim, we are relieved from the temptation to lower the standard to be aimed at to something which we may have a reasonable hope of attaining to simply by our own exertions. Thus, however far we advance, the goal lies far beyond, and we are kept humble by the sense of our grievous deficiencies.

But it is, perhaps, most of all in the feelings which it leads us to entertain towards God that Christianity goes so far beyond natural religion. The feeling of duty, the feeling that we must act in such or such a way, by itself alone is quite compatible with our looking on God as a hard taskmaster, with the absence of love towards Him.   I do not say that even pagans did not get beyond this.   The various provisions for our welfare which we find in the system of nature, in the construction of our own bodies, evince the care of God for His creatures, and tend to lead us to look on Him as a Father.   Still, the consciousness that we have done wrong produces a feeling of alienation from Him, and we can only hope that He may tolerate our transgressions if, on the whole, we try to serve Him.   This appears to be as far as we can be carried by natural religion.

But the Christian religion holds out to us a far brighter prospect than this, even a complete deliverance, in due time, from sin; and, meanwhile, during our earthly struggle, we can look on God as our Father, training us, if we will only lend ourselves to His training, and educating us for that high estate.

Moreover, that condition, as we are taught, is one

which is not to be terminated by death, and in which, accordingly, we may naturally suppose that there may be scope for the exercise of man's capacity for continued progress. If it be true that death was no necessary part of man's original condition, but that he became subject to it when he fell from an original condition of innocence—and the supposition that it *is* true explains, as we have seen, several anomalies,—then it is perfectly consonant to reason to suppose that if by any means he could be brought into a condition of uniform rectitude, that condition would not be liable to be cut short by death; and that it is not so liable appears to be a point on which all Christians are agreed.

The existence of physical pain, which belongs to the whole animal world as well as to man, regarded as involved in the system of things established by a benevolent Creator, is by no means free from mystery. We see, indeed, that it has useful ends, which it accomplishes, in deterring man and animals generally from doing things which might be injurious to their bodies. Still, it is in itself a source of suffering. The future condition which we have been contemplating is represented as being free from pain.

Thus, while Christianity extends beyond natural theology, and involves the admission of the supernatural, it, at the same time, harmonises with it

where the two meet on common ground, not de-
stroying, but fulfilling such aspirations as natural
theology leads us to entertain. Though natural
theology may go a long way in pointing out to us
our duty, it is to Christianity we must look for
the supply of those inspiriting motives with which
it furnishes us for the performance of it. Though
it demands that we shall accept some things which
are what we call supernatural, the different parts
of it, as it seems to me, dovetail into one another,
into what we learn from natural theology, and even
occasionally, to a certain extent, into matters that
belong to so different a thing as natural science, in
such a manner as to offer checks of its truth, which,
at least, commend it to further investigation.

In what I have been saying in to-day's Lecture, I
fear I have, to a certain extent, transgressed the
limits laid down for his lecturers in Lord Gifford's
Will. The idea he had in his mind was a lofty
one; but, as I said already in opening my first
course of Lectures, now more than two years ago,
not one which, for my own part, I think possible of
attainment in the way he indicated. I believe that
it is practically necessary to allow the lecturers a
good deal of latitude, and I have ventured to treat
my subject somewhat freely, I hope not to too great
a degree.

LECTURE IX

Man's craving after a closer approach to God satisfied through Christ—But not as yet fully—Christ as a perfect human example—Depth of a human character comes out incidentally—Instance in relation to the considerateness of Christ—To the firmness of His determination to do His Father's will—Limitation of our means of studying the character of Christ—Craving after a fuller objective knowledge met by the gift of an indwelling Spirit—Christian doctrine of the Trinity—Satisfies certain aspirations of natural theology—Christian foundation of a belief in a survival of death.

IN my last Lecture, since the delivery of which, I regret to say, a considerable interval has elapsed, I endeavoured briefly to point out how the Christian religion, supposed to be true, explains certain anomalies and supplies certain desiderata which are left by mere natural theology, how far soever we attempt to carry it. The feature of the Christian religion which I mentioned with special prominence was that fundamental one from which its very name is derived—the doctrine, namely, that a revelation has been made from God to man through a Being in whom the two natures were united. If this be true, we can readily understand what an enormous advantage it gives us over anything that we could attain to by the mere exercise of our natural faculties, even when among them we include the moral faculties. The idea of a God would seem to be almost instinctive in the human race, however low it may sometimes have sunk in uninstructed nations. Frequently it was degraded into polytheism of some kind; and even when the idea of monotheism was reached, or retained, it seemed so abstract that there was a strong tendency to seek in some way or other an objective realisation of the conception. This craving after something tangible, as it were, in the idea of a power above us led to attempts to satisfy it in various forms of idolatry. The depth of the craving, when no such unlawful attempt is made, but the monotheistic idea is maintained in its purity, is beautifully expressed in those words of a very ancient book: "Behold, I go forward, but He is not there, and backward, but I cannot perceive Him; on the left hand where He doth work, but I cannot behold Him; He hideth Himself on the right hand that I cannot see Him."

I have said that the desire, legitimate though it be, of being brought closer to God, when man attempts to satisfy it in a way of his own devising leads on to idolatry. And yet there is a legitimate satisfaction, within its assigned limits, of this desire. To a certain extent, we may say, that it receives satisfaction when a man, such as a virtuous pagan, meditates on the character of God, as shown "by the things that are made,"—His benevolence, for example, as shown by the contrivances for the good of the creature. But those who accept the Christian religion can get far beyond this by studying the character of Christ. Through One in whom the Divine and human natures are united, we are able through the veil of the humanity, and of the limitations to which human nature is subject, to get an insight into the character of the invisible God, and we have held before us for our imitation the example of a divinely perfect humanity.

And yet the satisfaction of the craving of which I have been speaking is not in our present state without its limitations. Christ gathered around Him a band of attached followers, but only gradually were they brought fully to understand all that He was, which they very imperfectly took in until after He had been removed from them, and their daily familiar intercourse with Him as Man had ceased. And the great bulk of mankind, who have lived after the time of His sojourn on earth, never had even this opportunity, and know Him as Man only through the memorials of Him that have come down to us.

In speaking of the endeavour to imitate the character of Christ, it might be said that I am going beyond the limits of the Gifford Foundation. Yet I do not think that this objection is sustainable. Those who believe that in Him the Divine and human natures were united, so that in Him as Man we behold the Divine perfection of humanity, will reverence and admire, and in their measure endeavour to follow, those features of character which beam forth from the records we possess of His life. But even those who believe Him to be only a human teacher acknowledge as a rule the loftiness of His moral teaching. Now example has a powerful influence in leading men towards that which is good, a greater influence, probably, than abstract precepts, however methodically arranged ; and even those who do not believe that Jesus of Nazareth was more than man, but allow, as almost all do, His moral superiority to other men, cannot but feel that His example must be deserving of the deepest attention.

If it be true that the true knowledge of God is life everlasting, and that Christ has revealed Him, so that the character of Christ gives us an insight into the character of God, according to the words that Christ Himself used—" He that hath seen Me hath seen the Father,"—then surely it behoves us to use such historical records as we possess for studying

the character of Christ.   If, indeed, He be what He
is believed by Christians to be, His advent on earth
was an event astoundingly supernatural, and it
seems almost axiomatic that the evidence of such a
thing must in part involve the supernatural.   The
consideration of evidence professedly supernatural
lies outside the object of the Gifford Foundation.
But surely we are not debarred from referring to the
memoirs which exist in the gospels, regarded as
simple history, merely on the ground that here and
there things are mentioned which *could* only have
been supernatural.   If the Gifford lecturers are
forbidden to *rely* on the supernatural, that surely
cannot mean that they are bound to *reject* the supernatural, and with it all that is in any way mixed up
with the supernatural.   The Gospel narratives may
surely be referred to as ordinary history.   Those
who believe that in Christ the Divine and human
natures were united will naturally read in His words
and acts something of the character of the invisible
God.   But the power of the words and teaching of
Christ is by no means confined to those who believe
in His divinity.   They appeal to the heart and
conscience, and have an intrinsic force independently
of any supernatural evidence.   What that must have
been to those who actually heard Him is strikingly
shown by an event recorded in the fourth gospel.
On one occasion, when the chief priests and Pharisees

sent officers to take Him, and they returned without
having accomplished their mission, and were taken
to task for it, they replied: " Never man spake like
this man." Even those who reject the divinity of
Christ, and regard Him as wholly human, allow for
the most part the transcendent loftiness of His
teaching, and of the morality which He inculcated ;
so that even for them it is an object of profound
interest to trace His character as far as our materials
allow us to do; though, of course, it is a very different thing from the interest of those who in Him
believe that they see an image of the invisible
God.

In many cases the lineaments of His character are
so plain that he may run who reads. But the
character of a man, whether it be of good or of evil,
but more especially of good, is often revealed in a
striking manner by something that lies altogether
beneath the surface—something so slight in appearance that it might well be overlooked, but at the
same time, when it is apprehended, gives an indication of what lies deep down in the character. I
cannot help thinking that we occasionally get some
such sort of glimpses in the narration of the words
and acts of Christ. I would offer an example
or two of what I mean, premising that I would
not presume in such a matter to give more than
a suggestion, which, whatever be thought of

the probability of it, may at least afford food for reflection.

One striking feature of the character of Christ is the extreme gentleness of the way in which He reproved faults in persons of a mixed character. I think we have an instance of this in the parable of the prodigal son. When the Pharisees and Scribes murmured because Christ received men whom they looked down on as sinners, and ate with them, He showed them by two illustrations the unreasonableness of their objection, and then went on to the parable I have named. In this the elder son is represented as objecting in anything but an amiable mood to the favour shown by the father to the returned prodigal. In the conduct of the elder son, thus worked up into the story, the objectors could hardly fail to see a reflected image of themselves. And yet there was no allusion to them, nothing calculated to wound their feelings, nothing of such a nature as to show to a bystander that it was aimed at them. The application was left to the silent voice of conscience in each man's breast, the whispers of which would not be stifled by resentment at any public exposure.

Another feature of the character of Christ, as disclosed to us in the Gospel narratives, is the absolute determination with which He set Himself to do His Father's will, cost what it might. To

those who believe that in Jesus of Nazareth the
Divine and human natures were united, this might
seem almost too sacred a subject to bring forward
in Lectures which were designed by the Founder to
be of the nature of scientific natural theology. Yet
surely the examination of a human character is
not forbidden by the exclusion, as evidence, of the
supernatural. I will venture, accordingly, to refer
to an assemblage of apparently unconnected inci-
dents, mentioned incidentally, in which, as it seems
to me, this feature is brought out in a very striking
manner.

We are familiar with the account of the Agony in
the garden, described in the first three gospels, but
not in the fourth. We see there, in the first
instance, what a real and severe oppression to His
soul the prospect was of what lay before Him; how
earnestly He desired that, if possible, it might be
dispensed with; and in the second place, how calmly
and absolutely He resigned Himself to His Father's
will when it became clear that thus it must be. In
the fourth gospel the Agony is not mentioned, but
we are led at once to the Betrayal. Here an
incident occurs which seems to indicate in a striking
manner the completeness of the surrender and the
firmness of the resolve. When He asked those who
came to take Him whom they were seeking, and they
told Him Jesus of Nazareth, and He at once replied,

"I am He," we read that they went backwards and fell to the ground. I am aware that some take this as an instance of some miraculous force proceeding from Christ. But it would seem better to take them with others as a natural effect of the words and manner of Him who spoke them, supernatural (to those who believe that He was more than man) only to the extent that they exhibited a human feeling, which as human is intelligible to man, with a perfection beyond what a mere man could attain to. According to this idea, the soldiers were taken aback and overawed by the majestic straightforwardness and fearlessness of the reply.

Shortly afterwards occurred another incident which, as related by St. John, gives an indication in the same direction. Peter began to use his sword in defence of his master, which Christ desires him to put back into its sheath, adding the words: "The cup which My Father hath given Me, shall I not drink it?" We have here the very expression used shortly before in that prayer of agony, which St. John does not relate; and the way in which the words here come in seem to imply a sort of disdainful rejection of the very idea of turning away from that cup of suffering which, at the conclusion of that prayer of agony, it was shown to Him to be undoubtedly His Father's will that He should drink.

Another feature in the life of Christ, and one

which He inculcated on His followers in such strong
language as to seem to us sometimes as almost
hyperbolical, is His perfect reliance on God's care.
This indeed is a feature closely bound up with that
perfect surrender of self which He exhibited. For a
readiness to give up life and all seems almost to
imply readiness to accept in minor matters whatever
may be sent. And yet how common are anxieties
about comparatively trifling matters. How eager
men are in the pursuit of money, to which they
trust for their happiness in this world. Now I need
hardly say that forethought is not forbidden, nay,
that it is easy even inculcated. But forethought is
one thing, anxiety is another. If we are directed to
look to God for our sustenance, it is not that we are
to expect to be sustained by miracle. We have our
part to do, but when that is done we are confidingly
to leave the result to God. It is not prudence or
forethought, but distraction, anxiety, that are forbidden when we are told to take no thought for the
morrow.

Example, as I have already remarked, tells more
persuasively towards following that which is good
than precept merely, and in the life of Christ
Christians believe that they have the highest possible
example. But perhaps, it may be said, "The means
we have for arriving at a knowledge of the character of
Christ are but fragmentary; if we had only lived in

the days when He was on earth, in how much better
a position we should have been."

But is it clear that we should have been in a
position more advantageous in all respects? In the
first place, the position which we have been imagining is one in which, we may say, no one has ever
been placed. It is true that Christ collected around
Him a band of disciples, specially the twelve who
had constant intercourse with Him. But it was only
gradually that they became aware of all He was;
nor does that seem to have been by any means fully
the case until after His crucifixion, when the familiar
intercourse that they had formerly had with Him
ceased. They therefore were not in the position in
which we have been imagining ourselves as placed.

But, in the second place, we may err in supposing that such a condition would be for our good.
This leads on to another of the fundamental doctrines
of the Christian faith, one of which some glimmering
may be traced in the minds of virtuous men who
have not had the light of Christianity. Christ is
reported to have told His apostles that it was for
their good that He should go away from them. He
was to be succeeded by another, not visible to the
senses, not one with whom they could hold intercourse as man with man, but a Spirit, dwelling in
their hearts, influencing their minds, leading them
towards good, and yet acting ordinarily in a way

which, like the invisible wind, is known only by its effects. This idea imparts a sort of awfulness to our lives, brings, as it were, God very near to our individual selves, keeps alive in us the sense of our responsibility ; while, at the same time, it encourages us in our conflict, showing us the all-powerful aid we have if we will only avail ourselves of it.

Perhaps it may be said, " How are we to distinguish this asserted action of a Divine Spirit dwelling within us, and influencing our minds, from the action of our own minds ? " But is it necessary that we should be able to distinguish ? Is it not rather of a piece with God's dealings with man, in his present condition, that there should be no such sharp objective realisation of the Divine presence ? But perhaps it may be said, " Surely when Christ was on earth He was palpably objectively present to His disciples." True, but this was in His human nature, and, as I said just now, it would appear that even the apostles did not become fully aware of all He was until after His crucifixion, when their intimacy with Him, as man with man, ceased. And St. Paul seems to indicate that there is a higher knowledge of Him than that clear objective knowledge obtainable while He was on earth. Writing to persons, many of whom were probably alive at the time of Christ's ministry, he says: " Though we have known Christ after the flesh, yet now, henceforth, know we

Him no more." The context implies that he regarded their present condition as an advance rather than otherwise.

There is thus in the Christian system a threefold presentation of the idea of God to the mind. We are led to think of Him as the first cause and fountain of all, whom no man hath seen nor can see. We are led to think of one in whom the Divine and human natures are united, so that, through the human and visible, we are led to such a knowledge of the invisible as the limitations of our human nature admit of. We are led to think of God as a Spirit dwelling within us, influencing our minds in a way which goes beyond what we can trace. Viewed from the side of man, this threefold presentation is a thing of which we can form some conception. But as to what it may be in itself, as viewed, if I may so speak, from the side of God, who shall dare to speculate? Have there not, both on this and on other points, been too many attempts to tie down the Infinite by the limits of subtle human definitions—to give humanly devised and unsatisfactory explanations of what is really beyond us?

In the study of the physical sciences we are accustomed to clear definitions and accurate reasoning. We lay the mind open simply for the pursuit of truth. Of course we meet with phenomena which we do not see our way to explaining; in some cases, we may see little prospect of our ever being able to explain them. In others we may think that an explanation is likely to be not far off. But in any case we do not profess to give an explanation, when the terms in which it is expressed are such as to carry with them no distinct meaning. Might not a similar proceeding be sometimes usefully employed in questions relating to theology? Might it not sometimes be better simply to say we do not know, and might not disunion be sometimes avoided with advantage by refraining from insisting on what cannot be clearly and intelligibly expressed?

The Christian doctrine of the Trinity bears in a direct manner on one of the subjects specially mentioned in the Will of Lord Gifford, as suggested as a suitable subject for discussion by the lecturers— namely, man's conception of God. I think it will be found to supply certain desiderata which are felt when man attempts, by his own unaided powers, to grasp the conception of God.

The various objects in nature suggest to the inquiring mind the question, How came they there? With respect to living things more especially, we can hardly entertain the idea that they have been as they are from a past eternity. And modern science negatives such an idea, not merely with respect to the world of life, but even as regards the inorganic framework on which life is sustained. The remark-

able phenomena of life seem to be utterly inexplicable, as a result *merely* of the forces with which we
are concerned in the inorganic world ; and the most
recent researches of science seem to have proved, in
so far as it is possible to prove a negative conclusion,
that life can only come from life.   Moreover, the
construction, more especially of living things, of
plants, of animals, of our own bodies, bears such overwhelming marks of design that we are led to associate
mind with our conception of a First Cause.   We are
led to think of a *Being* as the origin of what we
see in nature.   But it is not merely what we see.
We think; we carry on, it may be, a long train of
abstract reasoning, and in doing so we are not conscious of any action of our bodies which could in any
way account for the carrying on of those trains of
thought.   Yet there was a time when we ourselves
were not.   We read in history of events which took
place centuries before we were born.   We require
some origin for the existence of mind, as well as of
that material and living framework in which the
mind resides.   And yet we are, each of us, only one
human being out of perhaps 1,400,000,000 living at
once upon the earth, not to mention the countless
multitudes who have passed away.   And our earth
is only one of a brotherhood of planets which,
or some of which may, for aught we know, be the
habitation of other races of rational beings; and our

sun, round which the planets circulate, is only one
out of a countless multitude of stars, which or many
of which may, as analogy would seem to render
probable, be surrounded by planets like our own
sun, and those planets again may be the habitation
of living things, perhaps of rational beings.   When
we consider the vast extent of the universe, nay,
when we even restrict our contemplation to our own
earth, and the countless multitude of human beings
which it contains and has contained, and then think
of all this as originated by a Being, personal in the
sense of being or having mind, and not being a mere
abstraction of laws—when I say we think of such a
Being, we are overwhelmed by the immensity of the
conception ; we question whether such a Mind can
have anything in common with the human mind ;
whether we are not each one of us lost as a drop in
the ocean in the face of so vast a multitude ; whether
one of us by him or herself can possibly be an object
of individual care.

Here the Christian teaching comes to our aid.   It
does, indeed, represent God as One whom no man
hath seen nor can see, as dwelling in the light which
no man can approach unto.   But it also tells us of One
in whom the Divine and human natures were united,
who, being man, can sympathise with us, and be
intelligible to us, and who, being also God, can
exhibit to us the character of the invisible God,

in so far as the finiteness of our human nature can take it in.

But one desideratum still remains. When we think of God as the Father of all, we get lost in the immensity of the conception. When we think of God as revealed through One in whom the two natures were united, we can indeed conceive something of the character of God. We can understand, as we could not otherwise have understood, the depth of meaning in the assertion that God is love. But He, through whom this revelation of God was made, is no longer on earth, visibly associating with men, as for a time He did. The feeling might still be left that now each one of us is but an isolated individual, one of a vast multitude; is it possible that we can, each one of us, be an object of individual care? Here another point of Christian teaching steps in to our aid. We are taught to think of God as a Spirit dwelling in each individual, bringing thus the great God in close relation to our individual selves. Thus the Christian conception of God attains a completeness belonging specially to itself.

The ideas connected with this Christian doctrine are not of a nature to be anticipated by man with only his natural powers to guide him, and therefore belong to natural theology only in so far as to recognise the manner in which when suggested they satisfy what are felt to be desiderata. But it may even happen that in attempting to push to the utmost human reason in the endeavour to supply desiderata which natural theology rightly feels, she may outstep the limits assigned to her, enter into a region which does not properly belong to her, and in which we need guidance above man's natural powers, and may thus more or less fall into error; and that when the attempt is made to blend these conclusions with others which are accepted on the strength of evidence from a source above man's natural powers, the two may be found not naturally to harmonise with one another, like two liquids which are mutually soluble, but rather to form a sort of theological emulsion, causing a certain amount of dimness in objects which are viewed through it.

I have already, in a former Lecture, thrown out some hints of what, to my own mind, seems to be a case in point. I am inclined to venture to speak a little more plainly. I feel that I am here entering on delicate ground, since the subject is one about which controversy has arisen, and respecting which there is a widespread difference of opinion. This controversy, turning as it does mainly on the interpretation of what is involved in what professes to be a revelation made from God to man, is one into which it would be quite out of place that I should enter. It is lawful for me, however, as I conceive, to challenge the correctness of a conclusion supposed

by some to be deducible from natural theology, or
even perhaps to be capable of being established on a
purely metaphysical basis.

Few, I think, who are not secularists themselves
would dispute the danger of the influence on religion
and morality which is likely to be exerted by the
adoption of the belief that at death man comes to an
end for ever—that, in fact, death is an eternal sleep.
But if there be a survival of any kind, what evidence,
independently of revelation, have we got for it, and on
what foundation are we to suppose it to rest ?

By those who are not secularists it has most
commonly been held that man consists of two parts—
the body and the soul,—the latter being an entity
independently of the body, and as most commonly
supposed being capable of exercising the function of
thinking independently of the body. I need not here
enter into the question whether man's nature should
not be regarded as tripartite rather than bipartite, as
that I have already discussed, though in a somewhat
different connection, in the fourth Lecture of my
first course. A bipartite division will suffice for my
present purpose. What, then, apart from revelation,
is the evidence in favour of a survival by the soul of
the stroke of death, and what may we suppose to be
the foundation of such survival if survival there be ?

Of physiological evidence it is notorious that there
is none; nay, the well-known fact that the activity

of the mind, and even its exercise at all as we know it, are bound up with the condition of the body, is distinctly adverse, so far as physiological evidence by itself alone can inform us, to the supposition of any survival. As to metaphysical arguments, arising from a supposed nature of the soul, their weight to my own mind is simply *nil*. The one great argument for survival, so long as we restrict ourselves to natural religion, lies, in my opinion, in the apparent necessity for survival of some kind, in order to vindicate the justice of God in requiting men according to their deserts. A minor argument for survival is the teleological one, arising from the combination of man's capacity for continued progress with the prevention of it by death; an argument, however, the force of which disappears if we suppose that man is not now in the condition in which he was created, and in which, had he remained in it, his progress might not have been cut short by death.

If there be strong reason for believing in a survival of some kind, the question next arises, What is the cause of that survival? An opinion that has been very generally entertained is, that the soul is by its nature indestructible, and consequently immortal. The natural immortality of the soul is a hypothesis which would account for survival. But though there be good reason even from natural religion for believing in a survival of some kind, and

though, if the soul be naturally immortal, there must
be survival, the converse proposition, that if there be
survival the soul must be naturally immortal, is not
therefore in the least degree necessarily true. The
argument for survival rests not on a physical nor on
a metaphysical, but on a moral basis; rises therefore
to a platform above that of the merely natural; and
therefore we have no right to assume that the cause
of the survival belongs to the platform of the
natural; it may just as well involve the supernatural. By this term, however, I would observe
that I do not mean merely the exceptional and
miraculous, but I would include all that lies beyond
what our natural faculties and means of observation
suffice for our attaining a knowledge of. Hence,
in examining such sources of information as are
available for making out the conditions of survival,
we should approach the study with an open mind,
free from prejudice, and humbly ready to be taught
the truth. But what the result of that study may
appear to be, is a question which it does not behove
me as Gifford Lecturer to discuss.

I have ventured to go into some points of
Christian teaching more fully, slightly though it
was, than appeared to correspond with the ideas of
Lord Gifford in founding these Lectures. I said
already, in opening my first course, that I did not

think the intention of the Founder practicable in the precise way which he indicated. What, however, if I may judge by the terms of the Will, he would have chiefly deprecated is a narrow dogmatism, founding theological propositions on isolated texts, which themselves are first assumed to be infallible. I trust I have not fallen into this mistake, though how what I have said may be regarded by others is more than I can tell. Unless I deceive myself, my own sentiments lead me rather to take broad general views, leaving as open questions many things of which a definite settlement one way or other is frequently insisted on. It may be said that even in this very Lecture I have brought forward isolated texts, chiefly from the gospels. It was not, however, for the purpose of founding doctrines upon them; they were professedly used merely as suggesting trains of thought that seemed worthy of attention, though whether the suggestions thrown out commend themselves to my audience or not, is more than I can tell.

LECTURE X

IN this, my concluding Lecture of the Gifford series,
I propose to trace in more detail than I have done
before the influence on religious thought of a scientific theory, which, of late years, has come very
much to the front. I allude to the theory, if theory
it may be called, of evolution.

In former times there was a strong disposition, on the part of religiously-minded people, to refer various common observed phenomena to the direct *fiat* of an Almighty Power. In many cases it seemed irreverent to attempt to refer these phenomena, even in part, to second causes. Men got into the habit of regarding this direct reference as part of their religion. Nor did they stop here. So satisfied were they with the truth of their own way of looking at the thing, that, if some scientific man ventured to suggest the action of second causes, in bringing about the result, he ran a good chance of being set down as an infidel.

But truth is great, and will prevail. In matters of purely physical science, the operation of second causes in bringing about useful results (whether the mode in which they are brought about through causes of that kind is one which we can wholly, or only in part, follow) lies so near at hand that it cannot be overlooked. Yet, even in physical science, we have examples of the tendency of the habit of mind to which reference has just been made. Some of us can remember the time when any geologist, who, on the strength of sound inferences from observed phenomena, ventured to maintain a far higher antiquity for the earth than theologians were willing to concede, ran good chance of being denounced as an infidel. This, however, may now be looked on as a

thing of the past, and speculations are freely allowed
as to an evolutionary origin of stars, and planets, and
moons, without its being supposed that such speculations are in any way opposed to theism, or even to
Christianity. And the reason why there is no appearance of opposition seems to be that natural changes
taking place in accordance with laws, which have
been ascertained by long-continued physical research,
appear to be competent to bring about such a state
of things as that which we actually witness from a
supposed earlier condition of a simpler character.

When, from the study of inorganic nature, we pass
to that of living things, be they animals or vegetables,
we encounter phenomena which, so far as we know,
the action of the physical forces is quite incompetent
to bring about. There appears to be something superadded which, in a general way, we call life, though
as to what the nature of it may be we are quite in
the dark. Nevertheless, we observe some laws, or at
least regular sequences, in relation to these phenomena. These laws do not, however, carry with them
quite the same feeling of causation as those of pure
physics; at least, so it seems to my own mind; though
how far that may be due to the fact of my having
studied physics and not biology, is more than I can
say. I do not, however, think that the difference of
the impression made upon the mind in the two cases
is merely due to this circumstance. I suppose that

biologists, as well as physicists, would allow that we
know more about physics than we do about biology,
more at least of what is of the nature of methodised
scientific knowledge; for I am not making a comparison in relation to the number of mere isolated
facts. The relation of biology to physics, in regard
to the idea of causation, may be illustrated by con-
trasting our present physical knowledge with reference to some phenomenon with what it was at an
earlier stage of the study. Let us take for illustration the colours of thin plates. Newton embraced
the laws of the phenomenon in his theory of fits of
easy reflection and transmission. This was so far
satisfactory, in the way of a working hypothesis, as
that it enabled us to deduce the appearance presented
in any particular case from a small number of independent laws. But further than this it did not go.
I do not think that it carried with it the idea of
causation, or, at least, if it did it carried it only a
very little way. Of the independent laws employed
in the deduction, some were even opposed to what
we should have expected from the others. Certain
consequences of the theory are, as we now know,
belied by observation; but even before this was
known I do not think the theory would have carried
with it the same idea of causation as does the complete theory now known, which is furnished by the
theory of undulations. As far as I am able to judge,

the laws of biology, in so far as laws are known at all, resemble far more closely the laws used by Newton to summarise the phenomena of the colours of thin plates than they do the undulatory theory of light.

Nevertheless, it is likely enough that far-reaching biological laws do exist, which, in relation to the phenomena of life, are more or less analogous to the physical laws in relation to the inorganic world. If these were known, we should have a right to regard the phenomena which flow from them as *evolved*, just as we do in the case of the inorganic world.

But in the latter case, as I insisted in a former Lecture, when we have gone back in the chain of causation as far as we have even any probable light to guide us, we come at last to a point where we can proceed no further; where there is nothing to indicate even the probability of further progress, though, of course, I do not mean that we can demonstrate that further progress is, in the nature of things, impossible. We can only fall back on a First Cause; though, whether acting mediately or immediately, we do not venture to affirm.

Similarly, as regards the phenomena of life, if we knew more than we do of a causal origin of the phenomena which form the immediate subject of observation, we might be able definitely to present those phenomena to the mind as evolved under the action of known laws from a simpler condition of things. To this extent evolution would be not merely conceived, but demonstrated with more or less probability. And even though we are not able to proceed far backwards in this manner, yet we might reasonably enough suppose that if we do not see our way to proceeding further, that is only because our acquaintance with the subject is so very imperfect as compared with what we know of the inorganic world. We may suppose, therefore, with high probability, that an evolutionary process stretches far beyond what we can actually follow

Still, this gives us no right to affirm that the chain of secondary causation is illimitable, nor even to assume, except for trial, and to guide us in our investigations, that it necessarily extends beyond the point to which we have actually traced it. And though, as I have said, it is probable that it does, there is one consideration which seems to make it likely that, even in the nature of things, we should not be able to push our chain of secondary causation as far back in the organic as in the inorganic world.

When we pass from inorganic nature to the world of life, we ascend to a new platform altogether. There is no reason for supposing that there is any such thing as mind in plants; but when we ascend from plants to animals, we have clear evidence of mind and will, culminating at last in man, who not only possesses life, as do plants, but mind and will, of which we have indications even in the lower animals, and, in addition to that, intellect and conscience. Once we enter on the world of life we are led on step by step till we come to mind, will, conscience. May it not be that, in this ascending scale, we are brought nearer and nearer to the Supreme Mind— that we cannot travel so far as we could in the inorganic world ere we come to phenomena where second causes fail us, and we must rest content with referring phenomena to a Supreme Will?

Of course there is no objection to our assuming, *for trial*, that some phenomenon that we are considering in relation to living things is the outcome of some secondary cause, and trying to make out what that cause is. But that does not justify us in laying it down as an axiom that such a cause there must be, and assuming as the actual cause the least improbable of those that we can imagine, however improbable, absolutely considered, it may be. Such a mental habit, as it seems to me, has a tendency to shut out God from our thoughts.

And yet this is not necessarily so; for there are those who habitually look on evolution as God's mode of working. And in such cases the objection which might be raised to this way of looking on evolution as a necessity is rather one resting on philosophical than on religious grounds. It seems to be assuming too much to suppose that we are so well acquainted with God's mode of working that we can affirm that it always proceeds on lines similar to those which, to a certain extent, we have been able to follow in our study of nature.

But though the doctrine of evolution when pushed to an extreme may not be favourable to a religious tone of mind, yet on the other hand, when it is held so far as real evidence, or even probable evidence, fairly conducts us to it, it is rather, I think, calculated to exert a wholesome influence even in matters of religious belief. There is not unfrequently in the religious mind a tendency to refer matters, even of physical science, so directly to the will of God, as to substitute the supernatural for the natural, and to reject, or rather not venture to entertain, evidence which may be forthcoming, that such or such an observed phenomenon is explicable as a natural con-sequence of such or such conditions. If this be the case even in the inorganic world, still more must it be so when we come to the world of life; and as we ascend in the scale, and pass from mere life to mind, and from that to all that relates to the moral faculties and their exercise, the tendency to shut out the con-templation of stated laws and natural causes, and to resolve all into miracle or quasi-miracle, is greatly increased. The danger of this is, that it may lead

16

the mind so to confine its attention to the end to be attained—an end the attainment of which is believed to be in accordance with the will of God—as to overlook or neglect the means through which it is to be reached.

Now the physical doctrine of evolution has, I think, a wholesome influence in checking such a mistake. The theist must hold that all the phenomena of life, no less than those of the inorganic world, all the operations of mind, and even of the spiritual faculties, are alike the outcome of a creating and regulating Power; and if it be a matter of plain observation that in the inorganic world there are such general and far-reaching laws, he cannot imagine that in those higher departments of nature, considered as a whole, there is an absence of law, and all is arbitrary. The development of our animal frame takes place according to certain biological laws, and yet the completeness of the development depends on much that lies in our own power—on attention, for example, to diet, exercise, and so forth. Similarly, the development of character takes place according to what we may call certain spiritual laws, and yet we have it in our power to give a direction to that development. In the religious mind there is sometimes, I think, too much of a disposition to look to what, for want of a better name, I may call religious miracles—that is to say, to overlook what may be

called perhaps the natural growth of the spiritual
life ; so to think of the end to be reached as not to
pay sufficient attention to the means whereby it
is to be attained. But when I speak of a natural
growth, I do not wish to be misunderstood. What
I mean is, that, as in the natural world there is an
orderly sequence of cause and effect which we can
more or less follow, so we should expect to find
something of the same kind in the spiritual world.
I do not mean by speaking of natural growth to
exclude all that is what we call supernatural—all that
lies outside the region to which the term "nature"
is most commonly applied. There may be what we
may call a natural influence of the supernatural.
There are laws of growth in the moral and spiritual
no less than in the natural world. This is recognised by Christ Himself, when He compares the
progress of His kingdom to the growth and ultimate
seeding and ripening of corn in a field. The dis-
regard of this natural growth, even in things spiritual,
is apt to lead to the neglect of the use of means for
the attainment of the end, and to nourish a sort of
fanaticism.

But I can imagine an objection being here raised
on the alleged ground that this is teaching that a
man has nothing to do but to put out and trust to his
own exertions for any amount of spiritual advancement. But this conclusion by no means follows.

Though man be put in a position which, by himself, he never could have attained to for rendering his advancement possible, it by no means follows that the development under these more favourable conditions does not take place according to laws, as stated in their way as those of the inorganic world, or that he has nothing to do in the matter, and may neglect these laws with impunity.

When we speak of a phenomenon as having been brought about by evolution, it is important, for clearness of conception, to bear in mind that the term "evolution" does not designate a *cause* but a *process*, or rather the *character of a process*. The distinction will be made clearer by taking an example. Suppose, then, that we inquire how it is that the planets are kept in their orbits, instead of flying off into space as a body left entirely to itself must do. We find that there resides in matter a property of attracting other matter, which we call gravitation, and we speak of gravity as the cause of the retention of the planets in their orbits. Suppose, now, turning our attention in a different direction, we find good evidence from fossil remains, that, at a certain period in the past history of our earth, animals of the crocodilian type appeared upon it; and *that*, without any indication that we can find of a gradual change of type from types of the animals that preceded the crocodiles. Suppose, now, we put the question—How

are we to account for the occurrence of this new
type of animal upon the earth ?   One conceivable
answer would be, that we supposed that there had
been an exertion of a Creative Will out of the ordinary course of natural sequence, though how far out
of it, and how far in conformity with it, we do not
venture to speculate.   Another conceivable answer
would be, " In the breeding of pigeons and some other
animals by artificial selection, we observe a gradual
change of character in the animal, not, it is true, going
to any great length, such as that which separates one
kind of animal from another of a very different kind,
but still going some little way.   Again, a certain
amount of variation is capable of being produced in
an animal or plant by a permanent change in the
environment.   We may suppose that, by a series
of changes taking place *in some such way*, some previous type of animal was changed, until, at last, the
crocodilian type was assumed, though the reality of
such a gradual change cannot be established by the
discovery of transitional links, which we must suppose have not been preserved."   Such an origin of the
crocodilian type we should designate as evolutionary,
a term which we should not apply to that first supposed.   Nor is it even, as I conceive, essential to the
applicability of the term " evolution " that the change
in question should be of a gradual nature, provided
only that, if not gradual, it was still brought about

by ordinary natural causes.   Several years ago a great change was brought about very rapidly, almost quite suddenly, in the bed of the sea in the Strait of Sunda by the great volcanic eruption of Krakatoa. The cause of volcanic eruptions is still a matter of debate, but no one doubts that they are, in some way, brought about by the operation of natural causes; and that being the case, we should not, I think, exclude a catastrophic change in the bed of the ocean, produced by a violent volcanic eruption, from the category of evolutionary changes.   If we knew of any similar changes, catastrophic changes if I may so call them, in the type of an animal or plant referable to natural causes, which we do not, they would not, I think, be excluded from evolution; it is because any changes that we do know of, which are of such a nature as to bear some remote resemblance to a change of type, are very gradual, requiring many generations of the animal or plant for their accomplishment, that we associate evolution with slowness of change, and it is only in consequence of this slowness that the difficulty arises which is presented by the absence of transitional links.

But we might go a step further in our speculations.   We might suppose that the crocodilian type originated by natural selection, in accordance with Darwin's famous theory.   Here we have a conceivable mode (whether probable or not is a different matter), whereby such a change of type as that involved in the introduction of the crocodiles might have taken place. Natural selection, whatever may be thought of its probability, is a definite theory, which evolution is not. The assemblage of natural laws, which form the postulates in the Darwinian theory, constitute the cause to which the observed result is attributed. Of course the absence of any visible transitional links forms a difficulty in the Darwinian theory, as it must in any theory of slow change; but this is a matter with which I am not concerned, as I am not arguing in favour of the Darwinian theory, but merely pointing out the difference between a theory and a mere classification of what are deemed admissible causes for the explanation of an observed phenomenon.

It is only when evolution is treated as if it were a general theory of universal application that it comes into conflict with theism. It may be that all the phenomena that we observe in nature are brought about merely by the operation of ordinary natural causes from some anterior condition. But if this mode of derivation were a universal law, as we speak of universal gravitation, then that anterior condition must have been brought about in the same way from some other condition anterior to itself, and so on indefinitely. The generality of the theory, if we

treat evolution as a general theory, will brook no
exception. But as the exertion of will, whether it
be human will, or any other will that has the same
spontaneity as that of which we are conscious as
regards our own wills, is excluded from the idea
of evolutionary derivation, the erection of evolution into the rank of a general theory of universal
application does seem to me either to banish God
from our thoughts, or to reduce the idea of Him to
such an abstraction as to land us in a sort of
pantheism.

Perhaps I may make my meaning clearer by
means of an illustration. Imagine the earth to
move round the sun as it actually does, describing
an elliptic orbit with the sun in one focus, and with
such a varying velocity that a line drawn from the
sun to the earth sweeps out equal areas in equal
times, but that the planets described orbits altogether
different, in which those laws were not even approximately obeyed. On that supposition we should be
right in saying that the earth was impelled to the
sun by a force varying inversely as the square of the
distance; and we might substitute for the observed
orbit of the earth, and the place of the earth in it at
an assigned time, the orbit and the place which would
result from calculation, after assigning their proper
numerical values to a very limited number of what
are called arbitrary constants, and we might calculate

beforehand the place of the earth at some future time.
But we should have made no advance in explaining
the retention of the earth in its orbit and the laws
of its motion. We could not refer the existence of
this force, by means of which we were enabled suc-
cinctly to express the motion of the earth, to any
known cause, that is, refer it to any general property of matter. If such there were, the other
planets ought to move in orbits according to the
same laws as the earth, which, by our supposition,
they do not. The reason why, in the actual state of
things, we are justified in saying that we have explained the retention of the earth in its orbit, the
form of the orbit, and law of the earth's motion in it,
is that we have referred it all to a general property
of matter, whatever the explanation of *that* property
may be It is because we have referred the motion
to *universal* gravitation, to a force regulating the
motions of the planets as well as the earth, of the
components of a double star as well as the planets,
that we say that we have explained the motions. It
is this generality which allows us to speak of the
theory of universal gravitation. To constitute evolution a theory in a corresponding sense, we ought to
be able to assign to it the same indefinite extension
in time as we do to gravitation in space, in passing
from one body to another situated elsewhere. Even
then the two would not be theories in the same

sense; for while one is positive the other is merely
negative. The theory of gravitation specifies what
is; that of evolution merely excludes what lies outside the operation of the natural forces (to use the
word force in a very general sense) which are open
to man's investigation, but without specifying, in very
many cases, the particular process by which such or
such a result was brought about from an anterior
condition. It is only this assumption of indefinite
applicability which, as it seems to me, brings
evolution in its extreme form into conflict with
theism. But perhaps few persons push it to this
extreme.

I have spoken of some of the tendencies of the
adoption of the physical and biological doctrine of
evolution in its relation to religious beliefs. This,
however, is only one special theory, and it may be
well to consider the general influence of the tone of
mind fostered by the study of natural science, in its
relation to religious and moral questions.

Now the pursuit of natural science engages a
man pre-eminently in the endeavour to discover
what is really true. Of course, I do not say that
all truth belongs to natural science; there may be,
and we believe there are, truths, and very important
ones, lying altogether outside its domain. I am
speaking only of the mental qualities called into play,

not of the field of their exercise. In order to make
progress in natural science, it is essential to lay
aside, as far as may be, all prejudice, to keep the
mind open to entertain for trial, and to examine,
any fresh indication of truth from whatever quarter
it may come. There is another faculty also called
into exercise, which is akin to, but not identical
with, the preceding; I refer to the power of observation. Two men may be engaged in similar researches,
suppose experimental. Something, we will suppose,
casually presents itself which lies outside the question which they were putting to nature. In the case
of one of the men, the thing merely passes before
his eyes, and he takes no notice of it, his mind, it
may be, being absorbed by other matters. The
other sees it, notices that it is something unexpected and remarkable, and determines to follow
it out. It may be that he does so at once; it may
be that he thinks it better first to complete what
he is about, and he makes a memorandum of it as a
thing to be further investigated.

Now the same qualities of mind are called into
play in the examination of what is, or professes to
be, moral or religious truth. We should come to the
examination with a simple desire to arrive at the
truth; not influenced by the wish to agree with this
or that party, but ready honestly to adopt what, to
the best of our judgment, is true; not slavishly

surrendering our judgment to this or that man or
party of men, though, of course, ready to show all
due deference to those who, as we believe, are better
qualified to come to a right conclusion than we
are ourselves. This honest and yet humble pursuit
of truth, and absence of party spirit, is, I cannot
help thinking, promoted by the pursuit of natural
science, where the same qualities of mind are called
into play, though the field of their exercise is of a
nature altogether different. If adherence to party
takes the place of an honest following after the
truth, the result is almost inevitably dissension between those who ought to be united in the common
pursuit of truth, though it cannot be expected that
they should in every particular agree as to where
the truth lies. If adherence to party takes the
place of honest seeking after truth, not only is
dissension produced between those who somewhat
differ, but also error tends to get stereotyped.
Truth is one, but error is manifold; and if two
persons or groups of persons differ as to what
they believe to be true, one at least must be
wrong, and it is very likely, indeed, that there
may be errors on both sides: that each may be
right as to some item or items as to which the
other is wrong. If they would only compare
notes in a friendly, truth-loving spirit the force
of truth might prevail, and each might receive

benefit from the other, and harmony between the two be promoted.

But while, as I believe, the pursuit of natural science has a beneficial influence, even as regards matters belonging to a totally different sphere, it is, of course, possible that it may monopolise too much of the attention, and even, when too exclusively followed, may lead its votary to look down on truths which have to be laid hold of in quite a different way from that of the mere exercise of the intellectual powers. Furthermore, important as those powers are, they do not constitute the whole of the mind, and there is little play for the exercise of the feelings and affections in the study of natural science. Too exclusive a devotion to that one study may leave the mind highly developed and powerful as regards the powers called into play in that way, but, at the same time, dwarfed as regards certain other mental powers, which are equally important in their proper place. But this is nothing peculiar to the study of natural science; the same thing is liable to occur in a too exclusive pursuit of almost any branch of study; only, the particular powers which are strengthened or else dwarfed will differ according to the nature of the study thus taken up.

But if there is danger, on the one hand, that a man, whose main attention has been devoted to the investigation of natural science, and the exercise of his reason in the pursuit, may be disposed to underrate the evidence for truths which cannot be made out by the exercise of the human reason alone, but which have to be assented to on the strength of evidence, in part, it may be, supernatural, there is surely danger on the other that one who has been in the habit of accepting, almost without question, what he believes to have been taught on a higher authority than that of man may be too much afraid of exercising his reason—including in that term his moral perceptions—in the examination of the evidence for the supposed authority, and in the interpretation of what is supposed to be thus taught.   There is danger that he may pay undue deference to the opinions of his party, or of those to whom he may look up, and try to stifle a still, small voice within, leading him to think that, in some respects, the real truth is somewhat different; it may be from undue fear of himself; it may be from want of reliance upon God to lead him to the truth; it may be from the inconvenience arising from differing from those with whom he was associated. Thus, instead of weighing *the whole* of the evidence before him, and honestly deciding as best he can from the united testimony of all the witnesses, he is unduly biassed towards some particular opinion,

and so turns away from what is really the truth.
If what is supposed to be taught on the highest
authority is in apparent conflict, it may be, with
the conclusions of science, it may be with the
dictates of the moral sense, he is not arbitrarily
to select one of the witnesses as alone worthy of
credence, and reject the others, but to form the
best judgment he can on the united testimony.
Surely those words of Christ, " Why even of your-
selves judge ye not what is right ? " imply that we
are to use our moral sense in judging of what
professes to be true in matters of religion, even
though it comes from a source which we are disposed
to regard as more or less authoritative.

In training the mind in secular knowledge, we
have *instruction* and we have *education.* We have
to supply the mind with information from without ;
but the way in which the instruction is conveyed
makes a most material difference as to the effect
produced. The highest form of instruction is that
in which, while information is conveyed, the powers
of the mind of the pupil are *drawn out,* and called
into exercise. At the opposite pole we have that
form of instruction which is vulgarly called " cram."
I need not say how different is the effect of the two
systems on the mind of the pupil. In the one case
the mind is strengthened for the work of life, and
kept in a healthy tone, just as the body is by whole-

some exercise. In the other, the reasoning powers are stunted for want of exercise; the memory is loaded—might I not say overloaded?—with a mass of ill-digested information, a good portion of which is likely, after a time, to be forgotten; and if any question should arise as to the correctness of some item in this mass of professed knowledge, the man may be unable to defend it, and can merely fall back on the authority of his teacher, who, perhaps, may have made some mistake himself, or, perhaps, may have been misunderstood by his pupil.

But as the mere conveyance of information by itself alone constitutes cram, the injurious effects of which I need not dilate on, so there may be an error of a diametrically opposite character in the mode of instruction. It may be that the teacher looks on it as the one thing needful that the mental powers of the pupil should be brought into exercise, and so reduces the information with which he supplies him to just the minimum required for giving him something on which he can set his mind to work. A pupil thus trained may be well able to exercise his mind on some very limited subject, but his range is restricted, and perhaps he may be somewhat inclined to conceit, because he does not know enough to understand how much there is of which he is ignorant. Moreover, if he knew more, he

would have a wider range in which to choose some
subject of inquiry on which his mind might be
exercised; and even as regards the one subject to
which he has confined himself, his pursuit of it may
be less successful than it might otherwise have been
from his being unable to perceive the way in which
it is allied to other subjects. The best system of
instruction is one in which the conveyance of information and the stimulation of the pupil's mind
to exert itself, in the way we may suppose of
original research or in some analogous manner, are
blended in due proportion.

I have referred to methods of secular instruction,
and to what is generally admitted regarding their
effects, with a view to drawing an analogy between
that and advance in what we may call spiritual
knowledge. If it be true that man is possessed of
moral faculties, and also that a revelation has been
made to him of things that he could not have
arrived at merely by the exercise of his own
powers, it stands to reason that both should be
employed in his advance in spiritual things. If
he allows his moral faculties to lie idle, taking
everything on trust from his teachers, he gets into
a condition having some analogy to that of the
pupil in my illustration, who was merely crammed
with information. If, on the other hand, he proudly

17

rejects everything that lies outside his natural powers, determined to trust to them alone, he resembles the pupil who worked in such a confined field that he remained ignorant of much that was important, and even in his own field was not able to advance as far as he might have done had he availed himself of information from elsewhere.

Any divorce between natural theology and revealed religion is, in my opinion, to be deprecated. In the study of natural theology we are not to shut our eyes to such light as may be thrown upon the subject by revealed religion, or to refuse to entertain for trial some solution of a difficulty felt by natural theology on the ground that the solution in question involves the supernatural. On the other hand, in the study of revealed religion we are not to reject the exercise of the moral faculties in forming our judgment as to whether what is asserted to be revealed is really so, and is rightly interpreted. The refusal to use our moral faculties in this way would put us into a position somewhat analogous to that of the pupil in the case first supposed.

I have spoken of mental powers as exercised in the discrimination between truth and error in moral and religious matters. But it should always be borne in mind that there is something else concerned in the discovery of the truth besides the

mere exercise of the mental powers.   It is a
readiness to follow the path of duty when known.
This clears the mental vision for perception of the
truth.   And that it should have this effect we can
readily imagine.   For what is duty but that which is
right, and what is that which is right but that which,
otherwise expressed, is according to the will of God?
The more the human will is conformed to the will of
God, the more ready will the mind be to apprehend
the truth of God.   I have mentioned this merely as
an effect conformable to human reason.   But those
who admit the authority of Christ will hardly fail
to call to mind His own words : " He that doeth His
will shall know of the doctrine whether it be of God
or whether I speak of Myself."

I now bring to a close my second course of
Lectures, and take my leave of you as Gifford
Lecturer.   The conception of the Founder as to the
nature of the Lectures which he established was
a striking one, but, as I have already mentioned,
it is one which I hardly think it possible to carry
out in the contemplated manner.   As I intimated at
the outset, it was only this feeling that justified to
my mind the acceptance of the office.   I felt that
(in my opinion, at least) some deviation from the
plan mentioned in the Will was necessary.   Perhaps
it might have been better if I had not ventured to

undertake the office, but left it to some one whose
studies had lain in the direction of moral philosophy
or natural theology.　In consequence of my own
studies having lain in a different field, I fear my
Lectures have been rather wide of the mark designed.　Still, it may be desirable, as intimated in
Lord Gifford's Will, that the subject should "be
promoted and illustrated by different minds."

APPENDIX

EXTRACTS from the TRUST DISPOSITION and SETTLE-
MENT of the late ADAM GIFFORD, sometime one
of the Senators of the College of Justice, Scotland,
dated 21st August 1885.

I, ADAM GIFFORD, sometime one of the Senators of the
College of Justice, Scotland, now residing at Granton House,
near Edinburgh, being desirous to revise, consolidate, alter,
and amend my trust-settlements and testamentary writings,
and having fully and maturely considered my means and
estate, and the circumstances in which I am placed, and the
just claims and expectations of my son and relatives, and
the modes in which my surplus funds may be most usefully
and beneficially expended, and considering myself bound to
apply part of my means in advancing the public welfare and
the cause of truth, do hereby make my Trust-deed and latter
Will and Testament—that is to say, I give my body to the
earth as it was before, in order that the enduring blocks and
materials thereof may be employed in new combinations ;
and I give my soul to God, in Whom and with Whom it
always was, to be in Him and with Him for ever in closer
and more conscious union ; and with regard to my earthly
means and estate, I do hereby give, grant, dispone, convey,

and make over and leave and bequeath All and Whole my whole means and estate, heritable and movable, real and personal, of every description, now belonging to, or that shall belong to me at the time of my death, with all writs and vouchers thereof, to and in favour of Herbert James Gifford, my son ; John Gifford, Esquire, my brother ; Walter Alexander Raleigh, my nephew, presently residing in London ; Adam West Gifford, W.S., my nephew ; Andrew Scott, C.A., in Edinburgh, husband of my niece ; and Thomas Raleigh, Esquire, barrister-at-law, London, and the survivors and survivor of them accepting, and the heirs of the last survivor, and to such other person or persons as I may name, or as may be assumed or appointed by competent authority, a majority being always a quorum, as trustees for the ends, uses, and purposes aftermentioned, but in trust only for the purposes following : (Here follow the first ten purposes.) And I declare the preceding ten purposes of this trust to be preferable, and I direct that these ten purposes be fulfilled in the first place before any others, and before any residue of my estate, or any part thereof, is disposed of, and before any residue is ascertained or struck, declaring that it is only what may remain of my means and estate after the said ten purposes are fulfilled that I call herein the "residue" of my estate, and out of which I direct the lectureships aftermentioned to be founded and endowed. And in regard that, in so far as I can at present see or anticipate, there will be a large "residue" of my means and estate in the sense in which I have above explained the word, being that which remains after fulfilling the above ten purposes, and being of opinion that I am bound if there is a "residue" as so explained, to employ it, or part of it, for the good of my fellow-men, and having considered how I may best do so, I direct the "residue" to be disposed of as follows :—I having been for many years deeply and firmly convinced that the true knowledge of God, that is, of the Being, Nature, and Attributes of the Infinite, of the All, of the First and the Only Cause, that is the One and Only Substance and Being, and the true and felt knowledge (not mere nominal knowledge) of the relations of man and of the universe to Him, and of the true foundations of all ethics and morals, being, I say, convinced that this knowledge, when really felt and acted on, is the means of man's highest wellbeing, and the security of his upward progress, I have resolved, from the "residue" of my estate as aforesaid, to institute and found, in connection, if possible, with the Scottish Universities, lectureships or classes for the promotion of the study of said subjects, and for the teaching and diffusion of sound views regarding them, among the whole population of Scotland, Therefore, I direct and appoint my said trustees from the "residue" of my said estate, after fulfilling the said ten preferable purposes, to pay the following sums, or to assign and make over property of that value to the following bodies in trust :— *First,* To the Senatus Academicus of the University of Edinburgh, and failing them, by declinature or otherwise, to the Dean and Faculty of Advocates of the College of Justice of Scotland, the sum of £25,000. *Second,* To the Senatus Academicus of the University of Glasgow, and failing them, by declinature or otherwise, to˙ the Faculty of Physicians and Surgeons of Glasgow, the sum of £20,000. *Third,* To the Senatus Academicus of the University of Aberdeen, whom failing, by declinature or otherwise, to the Faculty of Advocates of Aberdeen, the sum of £20,000. And *Fourth,* To the Senatus Academicus of the University of St. Andrews, whom failing, by declinature or otherwise, to the Physicians and Surgeons of St. Andrews, and of the district twelve miles round it, the sum of £15,000 sterling, amounting the said four sums in all to the sum of £80,000 sterling; but said bequests are made, and said sums are to be paid in trust only for the following purpose, that is to say, for the purpose of establishing in each of the four cities of Edinburgh, Glasgow, Aberdeen, and St. Andrews, a Lectureship or Popular Chair for " Promoting, Advancing, Teaching, and Diffusing the study of Natural Theology," in the widest sense of that term, in other words, " The Knowledge of God, the Infinite, the All, the First and Only Cause, the One and the Sole Substance, the Sole Being, the Sole Reality, and the Sole Existence, the Knowledge of His Nature and Attributes, the Knowledge of the Relations which men and the whole universe bear to Him, the Knowledge of the Nature and Foundation of Ethics or Morals, and of all Obligations and Duties thence arising." The Senatus Academicus in each of the four Universities, or the bodies substituted to them respectively, shall be the patrons of the several lectureships, and the administrators of the said respective endowments, and of the affairs of each lectureship in each city. I call them for shortness simply the " patrons." Now I leave all the details and arrangements of each lectureship in the hands and in the discretion of the " patrons " respectively, who shall have full power from time to time to adjust and regulate the same in conformity as closely as possible to the following brief principles and directions which shall be binding on each and all of the " patrons " as far as practicable and possible. I only indicate leading principles. *First*, The endowment or capital fund of each lectureship shall be preserved entire, and be invested securely upon or in the purchase of lands or heritages which are likely to continue of the same value, or increase in value, or in such other way as Statute may permit ; merely the annual proceeds or interest shall be expended in maintaining the respective lectureships. *Second,* The " patrons " may delay the institution of the lectureships, and may from time to time intermit the appointment of lecturers and the delivery of lectures for one or more years for the purpose of accumulating the income or enlarging capital. *Third,* The lecturers shall be appointed from time to time, each for a period of only two years and no longer, but the same lecturer may be reappointed for other two periods of two years each, provided that no one person shall hold the office of lecturer in the same city for more than six years in all, it being desirable that the subject be promoted and illustrated by different minds. *Fourth,* The lecturers appointed shall be subjected to no test of any kind, and shall not be required to take any oath, or to emit or subscribe any declaration of belief, or to make any promise of any kind ; they may be of any denomination whatever, or of no denomination at all (and many earnest and high-minded men prefer to belong to no ecclesiastical denomination) ; they may be of any religion or way of thinking, or, as is sometimes said, they may be of no religion, or they may be so-called sceptics or agnostics or free-thinkers, provided only that the " patrons " will use diligence to secure that they be able reverent men, true thinkers, sincere lovers of and earnest inquirers after truth. *Fifth,* I wish the lecturers to treat their subject as a strictly natural science, the greatest of all possible sciences, indeed, in one sense, the only science, that of Infinite Being, without reference to or reliance upon any supposed special exceptional or so-called miraculous revelation. I wish it considered just as astronomy or chemistry is. I have intentionally indicated, in describing the subject of the Lectures, the general aspect which personally I would expect the Lectures to bear, but the lecturers shall be under no restraint whatever in their treatment of their theme ; for example, they may freely discuss (and it may be well to do so) all questions about man's conceptions of God or the Infinite, their origin, nature, and truth, whether he can have any such conceptions, whether God is under any or what limitations, and so on, as I am persuaded that nothing but good can result from free discussion. *Sixth,* The Lectures shall be public and popular, that is, open not only to students of the Universities, but to the whole community without matriculation, as I think that the subject should be studied and known by all, whether receiving University instruction or not. I think such knowledge, if real, lies at the root of all wellbeing. I suggest that the fee should be as small as is consistent with the due management of the lectureships, and the due appreciation of the Lectures. Besides a general and popular audience, I advise that the lecturers also have a special class of students conducted in the usual way, and instructed by examination and thesis, written and oral. *Seventh,* As to the number of the Lectures, much must be left to the discretion of the lecturer, I should think the subject cannot be treated even in abstract in less than twenty Lectures, and they may be many times that number. *Eighth,* The "patrons" if and when they see fit may make grants from the free income of the endowments for or towards the publication in a cheap form of any of the Lectures, or any part thereof, or abstracts thereof, which they may think likely to be useful. *Ninth,* The "patrons" respectively shall all annually submit their accounts to some one chartered accountant in

Edinburgh, to be named from time to time by the Lord Ordinary on the Bills, whom failing, to the Accountant of the Court of Session, who shall prepare and certify a short abstract of the accounts and investments, to be recorded in the Books of Council and Session, or elsewhere, for preservation. And my desire and hope is that these lectureships and lectures may promote and advance among all classes of the community the true knowledge of Him Who is, and there is none and nothing besides Him, in Whom we live and move and have our being, and in Whom all things consist, and of man's real relationship to Him Whom truly to know is life everlasting. If the residue of my estate, in the sense before defined, should turn out insufficient to pay the whole sums above provided for the four lectureships (of which shortcoming, however, I trust there is no danger), then each lectureship shall suffer a proportional diminution ; and if, on the other hand, there is any surplus over and above the said sum of £80,000 sterling, it shall belong one-half to my son, the said Herbert James Gifford, in life-rent, and to his issue other than the heirs of entail in fee, whom failing, to my unmarried nieces equally in fee ; and the other half shall belong equally among my unmarried nieces. And I revoke all settlements and codicils previous to the date hereof if this receives effect, providing that any payments made to legatees during my life shall be accounted as part payment of their provisions. And I consent to registration hereof for preservation, and I dispense with delivery hereof. In witness whereof, these presents, written on this and the six preceding pages by the said Adam West Gifford, in so far as not written and filled in by my own hand, are, with the marginal notes on pages four and five (and the word "secluding" on the eleventh line from top of page third, being written on an erasure), subscribed by me at Granton House, Edinburgh, this twenty-first day of August Eighteen hundred and eighty-five years, before these witnesses, James Foulis, Doctor of Medicine, residing in Heriot Row, Edinburgh, and John Campbell, cab driver, residing at No. 5 Mackenzie Place, Edinburgh.   AD. GIFFORD.

    James Foulis, M.D., Heriot Row,
      Edinburgh, *witness.*

    John Campbell, cab driver, 5
      Mackenzie Place, *witness.*

INDEX

The following Index applies to both of the author's courses of *Gifford Lectures ;* the first (referred to as i.) delivered and published in 1891, the second (ii.) forming the present volume.

Printed by R. & R. CLARK, *Edinburgh*

For EU product safety concerns, contact us at Calle de José Abascal, 56–1°, 28003 Madrid, Spain or eugpsr@cambridge.org.

www.ingramcontent.com/pod-product-compliance
Ingram Content Group UK Ltd.
Pitfield, Milton Keynes, MK11 3LW, UK
UKHW010345140625
459647UK00010B/847